HUMBER
AN ILLUSTRATED HISTORY
1868-1976

TONY FREEMAN

ACADEMY BOOKS

HUMBER
AN ILLUSTRATED HISTORY
1868 - 1976

Thomas Humber, 16th October 1841 to 23rd November 1910.

Humber - An Illustrated History
First published in Great Britain in June 1991 by Academy Books Limited
Copyright: A C L Freeman 1991
ISBN 1 873361 04 1

Printed by: Hillman Printers (Frome) Limited
Handlemaker Road
Marston Trading Estate
Frome
Somerset
BA11 4RW

Published and distributed by:
Academy Books Limited
35 Pretoria Avenue
London E17 7DR

Direct sales enquiries to:
Telephone: 081 521 7647
Facsimile: 081 503 6655

ACKNOWLEDGEMENTS

This book resulted from a telephone call I received from Stephen Lewis shortly after the release of *Daimler and Lanchester, An Illustrated History*. Stephen Lewis is Chairman and Historian of the *Post Vintage Humber Car Club* and suggested that a book on the history of the whole Humber marque would be an interesting project. This intrigued me and I began to make some enquiries. Although several books have touched on Humber, only Demaus and Tarring's excellent *The Humber Story, 1868-1932* had dealt with the subject in any detail. However, in this case most of the Post-Vintage Humbers under Rootes could not be included, given that book's self-imposed limits. Contact with John Tarring revealed that some newly discovered photographs had come to light after the release of *The Humber Story*. Stephen Lewis also confirmed that there was a wealth of material on the Post-Vintage Humbers, as well as taped interviews with senior Rootes management. Both the *Humber Register* and the *Post Vintage Humber Car Club* were prepared to allow me access to their archives.

My own family was involved in the motor trade from immediately before the First World War until the early 1980s. My paternal grandfather was a Morris distributor, but, it emerged, he also supplied Humber cars to some of his wealthier customers in the 1930s on an agency basis. This was a normal practice at this time, although fiercely discouraged after the Second World War as the manufacturers began to impose stringent controls on their distributors. My maternal grandfather traded from 1931 as a Singer agent prior to its absorption into the Rootes group. With a wealth of material, and a family connection, how could I resist such a project?

The contributions of Stephen Lewis and John Tarring, who arranged for many of the photographs in this book to be made available to me, and Brian Demaus, who was kind enough to arrange for prints to be made, were invaluable. All three of these gentlemen were of assistance in preparing the text, and were able to answer the many, many questions which I had in the course of my research, to go through the drafts in some detail and to make some very helpful suggestions on a number of points. Thanks are also due to J Reg Watkin, R J Evans, Reg Turner, Fred Taylor, Dr Roger N F Thornley, Bobbie Mitchell of the B.B.C., Graham Haswell, former managing directors of the Rootes group, the late E W Hancock and W Gardiner, Peter Ware, Engineering Director from 1958 to 1966, Michael Heath of the Humber development section, and Leon Gibbs and to Norman Garrad, former director of the Rootes racing programme, who was able to answer my questions on rallying Humbers. Thank you to Vernon Cox, Chairman of the *Salmons Tickford Owner's Club*, for arranging for his car to be made available for the photograph on the front cover. Matthew Critchley and Joan Williamson are also thanked for letting me loose among the Royal Automobile Club archives in Pall Mall. Peugeot-Talbot UK is thanked for it's assistance, as is Ralph Cartwright for uncovering some much needed research material on the 1950s Humbers, and Raymond Baxter, who was kind enough to contribute the Foreword.

Tony Freeman
April 1991

PICTURE CREDITS

J Reg Watkin Collection
1910 25 h.p. Monoplane 1914-15, Humber 14 h.p. Tourer with trailer ambulance, 1922 Humber office block at Humber Road, Coventry, 1922 Humber bicycle assembly shop, 1922 Humber showroom, Holborn Viaduct, 1922 Humber West End Showroom, 94 New Bond Street.

Dr Roger N F Thornley Collection
Humber stand at 1906 Olympia Motor Show, 1910 Humber 12 h.p. 4-seater limousine, 1910 16 h.p. Touring car

Brian Demaus Collection
1906 10/12 Coventry Humber, 1907 15 h.p. Coventry Humber in Palace Yard, Hereford 1920 15.9 h.p.

John C Tarring Collection
Thomas Humber, Humber, Marriott and Cooper, Thomas Humber and Thomas Harrison Lambert, 1899 Humber Motor Sociable, 1899 Humber quadracycle, 1900 1st Humber car, 1901 4 ½ h.p. Humber car (2 shots), 1902 12 h.p. Humber car 1903, 5 h.p. Humberette, 1904 6 ½ h.p. Humber car (2 shots) 1905 Humber Olympia Motor Tricar 1905 Humber catalogue cover 1907 10-12 Coventry Humber 4-seater tourer 1907 Isle of Man TT race 1913 Humber single seater sprint car driven by W G Tuck 1914 11h.p. 2 seater 1920 10 h.p. 2/3 seater 1923 11.4 h.p. 4 seater tourer 1925 12/25 h.p. Tourer 1927 9/20 Tourer (3 shots) 1928 20/55 h.p. 5/7 seater Landaulette 1928 9/20 Humber fabric saloon 1920s Humber works photos

B.B.C.
Humber Outside Broadcast Unit.

Manx Museum Collection
1908 Isle of Man TT
All other illustrations, courtesy of J M Alridge, E W Hancock and the *Post-Vintage Humber Car Club*.

CONTENTS

Foreword by Raymond Baxter   5

Introduction   6

1. Cycles and Motor Cycles   7

2. The Humber Motor Car   15

3. Quality and Style Before Performance   21

4. The Rootes Takeover   29

5. Humber Fighting Vehicles   46

6. Post-War Developments   53

7. The Series Cars   81

8. Decline   104

9. The Boulton Humber   112

Appendices

(i) Humber Chassis Types   116

(ii) Rootes Humbers   118

(iii) Humber Government Vehicles   119

(iv) The Post Vintage Humber Car Club   120

(v) The Humber Register   122

(vi) Other Humber and Related Car Clubs   123

Index   124

FOREWORD

Although I have never owned one, on reflection I realise that Humber cars have played a significant part in my life. During and immediately after the Second World War the occasional trip in the creme-de-la-creme of HM Forces' staff cars, the historic Humber 4 x 4, made a pleasant change from the more humble vehicles normally available to junior officers.

Subsequently, as an aspiring broadcaster, I lost count of the number of rendevous I kept with B.B.C. Humber recording cars.

Competing in the Monte Carlo Rally of 1953 the rugged construction of the Humber probably saved my life; and on the 1961 R.A.C. Rally my co-driver, Leonard Miller, and I, in a single entry, won a surprising victory against the redoubtable works teams in our Class.

It may not feature prominently amongst the legendary glitterati, - Bentley, Aston Martin, Lea Francis and the like - but the name Humber deserves its place in the history of the British Motor Industry. This book fully justifies that claim and redresses a long standing omission from the archive.

Raymond Baxter

Raymond Baxter

Raymond Baxter at the wheel of a Humber Super Snipe in the Prescott Hill Climb Special Section during the 1961 R.A.C. Rally.

INTRODUCTION

Thomas Humber first opened a pedal-cycle works in Stretton Street, Nottingham in 1870, following a period drifting from job to job. Immediately prior to setting up his own firm, he had been in the employ of William Campion, a manufacturer of domestic sewing machines, as chief blacksmith. Campion was an exhibitor at the Paris Exhibition in 1867, where he first saw the and bought new velocipedes of the Michaux type. Humber improved on the original Michaux design and by 1873, he had sufficient confidence in these improvements to market his own "Spider Bicycle".

The Humber concern prospered on the back of a fashionable cycle boom, which peaked by the mid-1890s and then declined. Humber then diversified into the manufacture of motor vehicles, largely through the influence of Harry J Lawson.

Lawson was a financier, who had made his first fortune during the cycle boom, and, with a keen eye on developments on the continent, where Karl Benz and Gottlieb Daimler had produced the first working automobiles in 1885 and 1886, he bought up every hopeful looking patent with a view to cornering the market in a new motor manufacturing industry. Amongst the patents he bought were those filed by one E J Pennington, an extraordinary American, who had strange and impractical notions about the construction and operation of motor vehicles. The early Humber cars and motor cycles were built under licence from his British Motor Syndicate under the Pennington Patents.

A crisis of confidence in the firm in the closing years of the 1890s resulted in the reconstruction of the company as *Humber Limited*. By 1901, the company was manufacturing motor vehicles of a more conventional pattern, and these early cars earned a reputation for quality which was to last until the final demise of the marque in 1976.

This reputation attracted the attention of the Rootes brothers in the late 1920s, gradually acquiring a substantial financial interest in the company. They carefully nurtured and developed the marque, giving it a quite distinct identity which began with the introduction of the Humber 16/60 and Snipe 80/Pullman and lasted through to the era of badge engineering in the 1960s. The Rootes Strategy was clear, Humber would appeal to the middle and upper classes and incomes, whilst the other Rootes concerns, Hillman and Sunbeam-Talbot, would cater for the volume and sports-car markets.

Rootes as a manufacturing combine dated from 1932, but their influence on Humber can be traced back to the late 1920s as a substantial minority shareholder and a majority shareholder by 1931. The commonly referred-to "Watershed" of 1932 came about when, in 1932, in time for the 1933 season cars, the Rootes manufacturing concern substituted side-valve engines for the long established inlet-over-exhaust designs which had been established Humber practice since their introduction in 1923. John Tarring, co-author of "The Humber Story" argues that this was, in engineering terms, a retrograde step, although there is no doubt that this achieved significant reductions in unit costs.

The final absorption of the marque into the Rootes empire has been placed at the 1933 model year by Michael Sedgwick, although the production records indicate that several thousand side-valved Humbers were manufactured in autumn and winter of 1932. The 1930s Humbers have been referred to as the "poor man's Rolls-Royce" and "the English Buick". The Humbers of the late 1930s were clearly influenced by American styling and they did offer good value for money. After the Second World War in particular, the reputation gained from the performance of Humber fighting vehicles was of solid, well-appointed reliability. Humbers were never particularly fast cars, but they were very comfortable and reliable, without being overly ostentatious.

This reputation resulted in Humber vehicles being the mainstay of the Royal Tours of the early 1950s and subsequently of the Civil Service and Government Departments through the 1960s and early 1970s. This achievement compares very favourably against Jaguar, who have long since replaced Humber as the supplier of ministerial vehicles. In the 1950s they could not have hoped to do this and had to purchase the ailing Daimler concern and maintain it as distinct marque to even gain access to this market. Despite their staid reputation, Humber cars were highly advanced, benefitting from a sustained post-war development programme that produced the first "Series" cars in 1957.

The demise of the marque can be clearly traced to the early 1960s, when the development of the Hillman Imp absorbed enormous amounts of money and management time which could, and should have been concentrated on developing markets where Humber, Hillman and Sunbeam were already established. Trying to build a car to compete with the Mini, which, it was eventually found, sold at a loss per unit in its early years, was unmitigated folly. On a profit per car basis Rootes did badly even compared with the British Motor Corporation, and BMC was hardly a model of profitability and management efficiency.

It is very unlikely that the marque will ever be revived. There was a tentative attempt to do so in the late 1980s, but with domination of Britain's luxury car market by the likes of Jaguar, Mercedes-Benz and BMW, the chances of any sort of commercial success are very slim indeed.

Tony Freeman
April 1991

1. CYCLES AND MOTOR-CYCLES

Born in Sheffield on 16th October 1841, Thomas Humber was the son of a tailor. His education was received at the Salthouse Lane School and his first employer was a Mr Cross of Mortimer Street, Nottingham. Although he was never formally apprenticed in Cross' trade of wheelwright and blacksmith, the young Humber learned quickly and was sufficiently skilled to forge the parts for some lace making machinery for Cross before moving to the Butterley Iron Company.

To widen his skills and experience as a blacksmith, Humber moved from employer to employer, but returned to Nottingham where he was employed as chief blacksmith by William Campion. Campion's firm was involved in the manufacture of parts for hosiery machines and was a manufacturer of chain-stitch sewing machines, which were exhibited by Campion at the Paris Exhibition of 1867. Campion's interest was engaged by the new French Michaux velocipedes, and an example was purchased and brought back to Nottingham. These were given to Humber who was instructed to make six sets of copy forgings.

Humber's early machines were made in his garden shed at 65 Northumberland Street, Nottingham and were sold purely on the basis of personal recommendation. He enjoyed some success as a small cycle manufacturer and moved to larger premises in Stretton Street in 1870. He moved again in 1875 to Queen's Road and again in 1878 to works at Beeston, by this time employing some eighty hands. Expansion at Beeston eventually resulted in the employment of some 2,000 hands.

Humber's first catalogue was issued in 1873, and advertised the Michaux-based "Spider Bicycle". Oddly enough, the early machines were not referred to as Humbers. It was not until 1874, some six years after Humber had commenced manufacture, that the cycle racing undergraduate, the Hon. Ion Keith Falconer, and not the manufacturer himself, is said to have applied the name *Humber* to the racing machines.

Another early customer, Frederick Cooper, was to play a leading role in the expansion of the firm towards the end of the 1870s, when, together with Thomas Rushforth Marriott, Cooper went into partnership with Humber. The triumvirate proved to be a powerful combination with Humber continuing to devote his attention to design and production, Marriott to the business administration and Cooper to sales and promotion. When in 1878 the business moved to Beeston, Cooper had also opened up a London branch in Lillie Road, where he spread the reputation of Humber as a quality manufacturer in the southern part of England.

Humber machines featured significantly in the racing successes of the new cycling sport. However, Cooper

and Marriott parted company with Humber and set up an independent partnership wholesaling tricycles which carried the Humber name. Unfortunately, Thomas Humber, lacking education and business acumen in this area, had taken no steps to protect his designs and patents and was left with little choice but to market his products as *genuine* Humbers in attempt to distinguish them from Cooper and Marriott's Rudge-manufactured Humbers.

As the cycle industry grew, pressure on space increased at the Beeston works and Humber once again acquired further premises, shortly after taking in Thomas H Lambert as a partner in 1885. Retaining the works at Beeston, premises were also obtained in Brickkiln Street, Wolverhampton, and at Lower Ford Street, Coventry in 1887. It is at about this time that the distinction arose between Beeston Humbers and cycles manufactured at other locations began to emerge, with the Beeston products becoming synonymous with the highest quality and a correspondingly higher price. In 1887, the business was formed into a limited liability company and Thomas Humber was retained as the general manager.

Lambert's influence, meanwhile was to lead to the introduction of Martin D Rucker, a former cycle manufacturer who was employed as manager of Humber's Holborn Viaduct premises and was later appointed the firm's general manager. Humber was by this time contemplating retirement and after his departure in 1892, the Humber concerns were to fall under the influence of Ernest T Hooley. Hooley was a financial entrepreneur who had successfully floated several companies in the public markets. He undoubtedly had considerable influence over Rucker, who was extraordinarily ambitious and whose lifestyle was beyond the means afforded by his position of general manager.

Under Hooley's influence an unprecedented programme of overseas expansion was undertaken, commencing with the flotation of *Humber & Co. (America) Limited* in December 1894 at Westboro, Massachusetts. This was followed by a series of other flotations and company formations in Portugal, Russia, Sweden and Denmark. Although the firm was one of the market leaders in the cycle industry in the mid 1890s, a severe crisis of confidence throughout the whole industry followed Hooley's bankruptcy in 1898. A direct result of this crisis was the dismissal of Rucker, whose extravagant lifestyle permeated his business dealings, as well as the entire Humber directorate.

The new board was faced with a formidable task. The shake-up which followed Ruckers's dismissal resulted in the appointment of Edward A Powell as Managing Director, whose brief was to restore both

1887. Thomas Humber and his partner Thomas Harrison Lambert on a Humber Tandem.

public and trade confidence in the ailing Humber concern. Notwithstanding that the Humber image had suffered badly from Hooley's bankruptcy, the cycle industry was undergoing a serious decline after the boom of the 1890s and the survival of the company required urgent and drastic management action.

Rationalisation of the production facilities was given a high priority with manufacturing being concentrated on the works at Beeston and Coventry. The various Wolverhampton works were closed and the range of products was revised. The majority of the Hooley-formed overseas subsidiaries were disbanded and the UK company was re-formed as *Humber Limited* in 1900.

With the decline of cycling as a fashionable pastime for the wealthy the company could not look forward to increased sales of it's relatively exclusive and expensive cycles. Cycling had become more commonplace and although the racing machines manufactured by Humber enjoyed an enduring popularity, the cycle was becoming a utility rather than a leisure vehicle. This was recognised by the Board as motoring became increasingly popular. Cycle production continued, although little effort appears to have been made to develop the company's range of cycles up to the outbreak of war in

1914. By the time production was resumed in 1919, the range of cycles had been reduced, prices increased and the directors of the company clearly felt that the future of the company lay in the production of motor vehicles. With the increasing influence of the Rootes brothers in the late 1920s, the cycle business was disposed of, the Humber transfer being licensed to Raleigh.

Humber's involvement in the motor cycle trade can be traced back to Harry J Lawson. Lawson's reputation in the 1890s was that of a financial entrepreneur who attempted to corner the market in the fledgling British motor industry. He was particularly known for his flotation of the Daimler concern in February 1896, which sought to capitalise on the Gottleib Daimler patents bought from Frederick Simms and his syndicate (See *Daimler and Lanchester -An Illustrated History* by the same author). Lawson's first fortune had been made in the cycle and related industries. Born in 1852 in Brighton, he was educated at Stephenson's Mechanical Institution and early in his career helped his father, an erstwhile puritan preacher, in the construction of models of Stephenson's equipment. Becoming involved in the bicycle trade in his native Brighton, in 1874 he designed a "safety" bicycle, reputedly the first with a chain to the rear wheel.

Moving to Coventry, Lawson was a key figure in the city's cycle industry in the 1870s, becoming manager of the *Tangent and Coventry Cycle Company*. Although he later ceased to be a manufacturer, he continued to design bicycles and in 1884, approached BSA, who turned down his designs. At this stage Lawson changed career, and became a cycle industry financier, although he did retain a number of connections which would prove useful to him later when he became involved in the motor car industry. Amongst these was Henry Sturmey, inventor of the *Sturmey-Archer* gearchange, who later founded *The Autocar* magazine in 1895.

With the cycle boom reaching its peak in the mid 1890s, Lawson converted cycle and tyre companies from private to public companies in a series of flotations in 1894 and 1895. This made him a substantial fortune which he began to invest in motor car patents. Anticipating that the motor vehicle would replace the horse as the main source of private transport, Lawson was quick to realise that the motor industry had the potential to become a major manufacturing force and reasoned that

Two examples of early Humber cycles, the 62 inch Humber Ordinary and the 26 inch "Bourdon".

Left to right, T R Marriott, Thomas Humber and Fred Cooper. The fourth man is T Ackroyd.

Humber bicycle advertising.

On Pleasure Bent!

A COUNTRY lane, a glorious day, and a man and a maid on pleasure bent!

There's no cycling quite like Humber Cycling. No other machine gives such easy and silent running, exhilarating in its buoyancy, thrilling in its speed.

Choose any model of the wide Humber range—superb "Beeston," famous "All-Weather-de-Luxe," popular "Olympia" or "Road Racer"—each is supreme in its class, with *Quality* the only standard.

Write to-day for handsome Art Catalogue.

Ride as you pay!

10/10d. down brings you any of these models:—The 'Cob,' 'Olympia,' or 'Light Roadster.' No Deposit, Free Carriage and Insurance.

New Season's models include:—
"Beeston" £14 14 0
"Standard" £10 0 0
"All-Weather de Luxe" £8 8 0
"Popular" £8 0 0
"All-Weather" £7 17 6
"Road Racer" £7 5 0
Prices from £5-19-6 to £15-4s.

Humber CYCLES

HUMBER LTD., COVENTRY. *London Depot:* 32, Holborn Viaduct, E.C.I.

251,338

MR. Harold Freeman, of Malvern Wells, has ridden more than a *quarter of a million* miles by bicycle—mostly on Humbers.

With one "Beeston Humber" alone, Mr. Freeman has done over 60,000 miles. Just with an ordinary sweet-running, everlasting Humber Cycle, such as you or I would buy this Easter.

BEESTON HUMBER CYCLE, fitted with Three-speed Gear, Oil Bath Gearcase, 1¼ in. Dunlops and Brooks Saddle. £15 12 6.

As supplied to His Majesty, King George V.

HUMBER, LTD., COVENTRY.
London: 32, Holborn Viaduct, E.C.
Southampton: 27, London Road.
AGENTS EVERYWHERE.

1899 Humber Motor Sociable

because of the relatively high level of technology used, would be dependent on a number of patented designs and processes, particularly those relating to the internal combustion engine. Lawson therefore reasoned that any individual who had control of the patents, as well as land, plant and finance, would stand to make a very large sum of money from other's endeavours.

In 1895 Lawson registered the *British Motor Syndicate Limited* as the first stage in his plan to "corner the market". The main object of this company was to buy up all past, present and future patents in the expectation of running across some "master" patents. This was an ambitious and expensive plan flawed by the fact that no such master patents existed, with the result that extravagant sums of money were expended on patents with little engineering merit and doubtful commercial value. The plan was intellectually sound in that the control of patents could have resulted in the flow of fees and royalties and dividends to Lawson and his backers. However, Lawson was insufficiently skilled as an engineer to discriminate between the few valuable and practical patents available and the many dubious patents offered to him. The fundamental flaw was that a patent in itself is merely a precise technical description of a process or design. It carries no warranty as to whether the execution of the design is commercially viable or practical. This weakness in Lawson's scheme was to eventually lead to the failure of his ambitious plans.

Following the formation of the British Motor Syndicate by Lawson, E T Hooley and Martin Rucker, with a share capital of £150,000, an option was purchased for £30,000 on a 12-acre site in Coventry where a new factory had been recently built, but was now disused. Several companies occupied premises on this site, now known as the "Motor Mills" the most prominent being Humber and the newly formed Daimler. Of the remaining funds, Lawson paid some £100,000 for some American patents owned by one Edward Joel Pennington of Indiana, which, along with some 70 or 80 other patents now owned or controlled by the Lawson syndicate, would form the basis for Lawson's motor manufacturing empire.

Pennington was probably one of the very few men who was able to get the better of Lawson. Born in 1858 in Franklin Township Indiana, Pennington had a colourful career and was described as *"the company promoter and charlatan par excellence of the horseless carriage era"*. Pennington left his native United States, taking with him a number of idiosyncratic designs for horseless carriages and internal combustion engines. By the time he arrived in London, Pennington had made contact with Rucker, who was the first in Britain to see these designs. Rucker felt that the patents were overpriced for Humber but nevertheless introduced Pennington to Lawson.

Lawson's subsequent purchase of the Pennington patents, probably on Rucker's advice, was a serious commercial error. A clear example of this was that Pennington claimed that his engines had a better power-to-weight ratio and were cheaper and easier to build. The Pennington engine, it was claimed, required no carburettor and no cooling system, jackets were made of steel tubing but with no cooling radiator fins but, it was claimed, could run indefinitely without overheating. Petrol was fed directly into the mouth of the induction pipe from the tank, the flow controlled by a needle valve. On the suction stroke, air and liquid petrol would enter the cylinder where a spiral of heated wire would vaporise the petrol. By vaporising, the temperature would drop

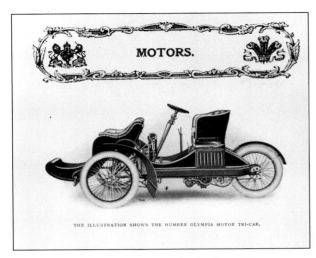

1905 Humber Olympia Tricar with wheel steering.

and the cylinder would be cooled. Further vaporisation would be brought about at the end of the compression stroke by a series of small sparks, and at the extremity of the stroke a larger spark would fire the charge in the usual way.

Pennington argued that by vaporising the fuel inside the cylinder, rather than the carburettor, the cylinder would be kept cool; thus expensive carburettors, cooling fins, water jackets and pumps could be dispensed with. Granted, the Pennington engine worked, but was lamentably inefficient. The amount of petrol needed to produce the cooling effect so enriched the mixture that it caused constant fouling. Pennington engines kept cool long enough for short demonstrations, but there is no evidence that they ran any distance. Pennington later fitted water jackets around his cylinders and used conventional ignition systems, but kept very quiet about it.

However, despite the dubious value of Pennington's designs, Lawson was still able to licence some of the Pennington patents to Humber, which were subsequently used in the early motor cycles and motor cars. With the importing of cheap American cycles in the late 1890s and the general malaise in the British cycle industry affecting the whole of Coventry's motor indus-

try, the Humber board had already taken the decision to diversify and in 1896 became the first British manufacturer to commence motor cycle production.

The Autocar of 16th May 1896 announced that Humber would have a display at the International Horseless Carriage Exhibition of *"motor cycles fitted with the Kane-Pennington motors and two tandem safeties with the two-cylinder motors boomed out at the rear.."* On 6th June 1896, a further report stated that: *"the first practical motor cycle built in this country was completed last week when Humber and Co. finished a bicycle fitted with a Pennington two-horsepower made at their works in Coventry"*. The engines for these machines were very crudely constructed, and the only remaining example in Britain is a tricycle with the Humber transfer.

In 1896, Lawson had paid Leon Bollee £20,000 for the English patent and manufacturing rights for the *Bollee Voiturette,* which was subsequently built under licence by Humber. This was a sounder investment. These Voiturettes were powered by a Bollee designed engine, which although liable to overheat, was reasonably efficient, generating 3 h.p. As a result, the 4 cwt. Voiturette was capable of nearly 30 m.p.h., 8-10 m.p.h. faster than the contemporary Panhard and twice as fast as the Benz. The Humber 1898 season catalogue carried several of these strange machines which were described as a *"Three Wheel Motor Carriage for three riders"*. This arrangement consisted of a two seater forecar which was little more than an extended pedal cycle frame with a motor mounted behind the saddle pillar. The claimed speed for this vehicle was forty miles per hour, although it is extremely doubtful whether this was ever achieved other than downhill with a fair following wind. A further offering based on the Leon Bollee designs was the *Motor Sociable,* so named because the seating was side-by-side rather than the tandem arrangement.

In 1898, the dismissal of Rucker and the scandal that surrounded the Hooley bankruptcy case resulted in the decision being taken to halt motor cycle production. When this resumed in 1902, the Humber company presented a design based on the Phelon and Moore

Humber bicycles.

5 ½ h.p. TT Model from 1919.

engines, which were bought in from Cleckheaton, Yorkshire. These machines had a 1½ or 2 h.p. motor which was engaged by pedal action. In line with Humber practice, a Beeston-manufactured version and a Coventry "Standard Special" version were produced, being priced at £60 and £50 respectively. These early motorcycles were well received and notched up an enviable list of competition successes in Britain and on the Continent. In particular, Humber works riders J F Crundall and Bert Yates achieved a number of successes on road and track.

These Phelon and Moore machines were further developed in 1¾ h.p. and 2¾ h.p. form and were fitted with a clutch in 1903. The 2¾ h.p. engine was also fitted to a tricycle and the Olympia Tandem Three-Wheeler was developed over the following years with the introduction of water cooling, hand-starting, two gears and coach-built fore-carriages. As the three wheelers became heavier, wheel steering was adopted, but the popularity of small tricycles declined as both motor cars and motor cycles became more popular and 1905 was the last year that these unusual cycles were offered.

A break in motor cycle production took place until 1909, when it was resumed and then continued to be an integral part of the Humber business until 1930. In 1909, only one machine was offered, a 3½ h.p. single cylinder model with air cooling and an exhaust silencer incorporated in the cycle frame. In 1910, this machine underwent a number of important modifications and an additional new 2 h.p. model was introduced which was then to continue virtually unmodified until 1914. This lightweight single was keenly priced at £35 with various cost options such as the Armstrong three-speed hub gear at 10 guineas and a free engine hub at £4. A Lady's model with a dropped frame and a gearcase for the pedalling gear was also offered at £40, with similar options at similar prices.

Additions to the range resulted in the production of a 2 h.p. lightweight, a 2¾ h.p. V-Twin and a 3½ h.p. single being offered in 1912. By this time the motorcy-cle side car was becoming popular and the 3½ h.p. model was offered with a choice of cane, wicker, coachbuilt or commercial sidecars. This range was modified and improved through 1913 and 1914 and supplemented in 1913 with an unusual three-cylinder opposed twin 6 h.p. machine specifically designed for sidecar work. These were not much of a success. Only one batch was made and their only legacy appears to be an article in a September 1953 edition of *The Motor Cycle*.

A works-backed sporting programme was re-introduced in 1910, with Humber Limited officially entering a team for the Tourist Trophy ("TT") races in the Isle of Man where P J Evans succeeded in winning the Junior TT riding a 2¾ h.p. V-twin model.

With the outbreak of the First World War, motor cycle production did not immediately cease. New models were introduced in 1915 and 1916 but civilian motor cycle production was suspended until 1919. In 1920 a new flat-twin 4½ h.p. machine was introduced. With a bore and stroke of 75mm and 68mm respectively, a capacity of 600cc was achieved and this relatively quiet

Humber 4 ½ h.p. model.

12

Humber bicycle assembly shop.

and refined machine was marketed as the "Silent Humber". By 1923, another new model was available, a 349cc single side-valve lightweight available in Touring and Sports versions. A side-car version was introduced in 1925, but by this time the decision had been taken to make this the only model available. Despite being refined and well-built machines, production was phased out in 1930 although a push-rod overhead valve version was added in 1927 and an overhead camshaft version in 1928.

The cessation of motor cycle production by Humber has been attributed to the Wall Street crash and the general belt-tightening that followed. However, it is more than likely that this was a decision made under the influence of the Rootes brothers, who were becoming more influential in the direction of the company as shareholders. Rootes had no interest in Humber's cycle and motor cycle operation, and the sale of the cycle manufacturing business to the Raleigh company and the winding down of the motorcycle operation freed money and management resources to concentrate on car production. It is also worth drawing a parallel with the fate of the British motor cycle industry itself in the late 1960s and early 1970s. Humber was able to build powerful and well-engineered machines, but, like the British motor cycle industry itself forty years on, was unable to compete effectively because of high prices and lack of technical innovation.

4 ½ h.p. motorcycle with Grindley sidecar.

13

Humber's showroom at 32 Holborn Viaduct, circa 1922.

The interior of the showroom. Illustrated are a 4 ½ h.p. twin motorcycle, both touring and sports models, 11.4 h.p. tourers and saloon and a BR2 rotary aero-engine

2. The Humber Motor Car

Following the purchase of the expensive Pennington patents in 1896, Harry J Lawson had more than a passing interest in stimulating interest in motoring. Several problems faced Lawson at this time, the first and most difficult being the legislative regime, which in early 1896 was still governed by three pieces of legislation, *The Locomotive Act of 1861, The Locomotive Act of 1865* and *The Highways and Locomotives (Amendments) Act of 1878.* Collectively known as the Red Flag Acts, this legislation had been put on the statute books at the prompting of powerful interests, particularly the railway companies and landowners, who had perceived a threat to their financial security when experimental road-going steam carriages had re-appeared at the beginning of the 1860s.

Fortunately, Lawson was assisted by Frederick Simms and the Honourable Evelyn Ellis of Daimler, who introduced the Canstatt—built Daimler motor cars to the Prince of Wales at a private demonstration in May 1896. The Prince, suitably impressed, was able to generate a fashionable interest in motor vehicles amongst influential parts of society, and it is no coincidence that the Red Flag Acts were repealed and replaced by *The Locomotive on the Highways Act of 1896*, which although still restrictive, did enable early motorists to make some practical use of their vehicles.

Another problem was the Pennington patents bought so extravagantly following Pennington's introduction by Rucker. Many of these were clearly impractical and although Pennington had been plausible enough, he probably had little clear conception of what was required in engineering terms to produce a sound and workable motor vehicle. This was hardly surprising. Few of Lawson's contemporaries had formulated any clear ideas about the long term future of the motor car. Even Frederick Lanchester, who is credited with the construction of the first all-British petrol-driven, four-wheeled motor vehicle in 1895, and who was one of the more advanced thinkers in engineering circles in 1890s Britain, had little idea that the petrol-driven motor vehicle would eventually replace the railway as the main means of public and commercial transport and the horse as the main means of private transport.

Pennington's designs have been described as "weird and wonderful" and "unconventional". What was without doubt is that vehicles based on these designs did not sell and Lawson's *Motor Manufacturing Co.* lasted but two years, finally folding because of *"the management fixation with producing Pennington's motorcycles, fire engines and other unconventional vehicles"*. Humber, constrained by Pennington's impractical designs, suffered similar problems and made little progress with the manufacture of his cars. Probably the entire production run amounted to no more than 15 vehicles,

The first Humber car produced in Coventry, May 1900.

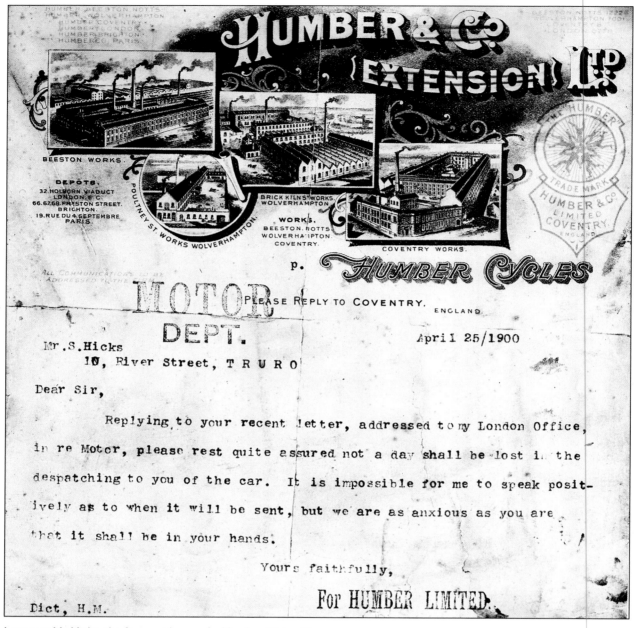

Letter to Mr Hicks, the first purchaser of a Humber Motor Car.

none of which attracted private buyers. Even the Bollee-designed tricars, some of which were powered by the Kane-Pennington engines, had shortcomings which became even more apparent with the arrival of the more conventional De Dion-Bouton engines in late 1896. Although attempts were made by several British firms to manufacture Pennington designs, the sole survivor bears the Humber transfer.

On 17th July 1896, Humber's Lower Ford Street works in Coventry, only completed as recently as 1887, burned down, destroying the company's motor vehicle manufacturing capacity overnight and resulting in over £100,000-worth of damage. Ironically, the Fire Service in Coventry, which attended the fire, had at that time been undergoing trials with a "Pennington Special" supplied by the *Great Horseless Carriage Company,* but this design, again, proved to be of no practical use. With overwhelming financial and management problems, no plant and vehicles which were unsaleable, the

Humber company could well have collapsed at this time, but with the decline of the cycle industry, the banks in Coventry had lost much business and were more accommodating to the ailing firm than would have been the case in many areas of the country at the time.

With the departure of Martin Rucker, Edward Powell's board had to make significant economies and to retain some remarkably able managers, amongst them Walter J Phillips, formerly of Rudge Cycles. Following the retirement of Thomas Humber in 1892, Phillips' influence had resulted in some experiments with motor vehicles prior to Lawson's involvement, including the construction of a prototype electric car in 1895. Phillips was also instrumental in bringing about the reconstruction of the Coventry works in a very short time during 1897, and in setting up a commercially viable motor manufacturing plant by the end of 1898. In the meantime, production of cycles continued in temporary premises in Coventry, first in Parkside and then in Priory

Street, pending the rebuilding of the Lower Ford Street works.

Following the arrival of the De Dion-Bouton engine the decision was made by Humber's management to drop the Pennington designs once and for all, a course taken by a number of other firms at virtually the same time. Harry Lawson, now faced with promoting products which were clearly of little value, resorted to litigation, claiming for damages and payments relating to infringements of his "master patents" and became embroiled in a series of lawsuits involving Humber and other firms for some years. By 1903, a receiver had been appointed to Lawson's companies and by 1904, he found himself indicted for conspiracy to defraud, and was sentenced to serve one year's hard labour. In any event, the newly reconstructed Humber company was finally awarded damages against Lawson in 1900, and the way was now clear to proceed with a corporate strategy unhindered by Lawson's deteriorating reputation and Rucker's discredited policy.

The board proceeded with plans to reconstruct the legal and financial structure of the company and on 8th March 1900, this resulted in the formation of a new company, Humber Limited. The new Humber company was financed by an issued share capital of £500,000 and following the closure of Hooley and Rucker's overseas subsidiaries and the Wolverhampton works, the large part of motor vehicle operations was moved to Coventry, now unfortunately known as the town of *"Three Spires, Dunlop Tyres and Humber Fires"* following another fire, this time at the Priory Street works. Motor car production, although mainly concentrated in Coventry, was also commenced at the Beeston factory, with price differentials between Beeston and Coventry products being introduced along the lines of the company's practice with bicycles, the Beeston products being more expensive.

In 1900, a Humber car which had probably been made in late 1899 at these works was delivered by road over a period of two days to their first private customer, a Mr Hicks, an ironmonger in Truro who had purchased the vehicle to re-sell to his customer, a Mr George

THE HUMBER CAR.

Net Cash Price	Standard	.... £275.
	Modele de Luxe	300 Guineas.
	(See page 2.)	

Catalogue illustration of a 1901 4 ½ h.p. Humber.

Powell. This is more than likely the car described in Humber's 1903 catalogue as a *"large car of the belt driven type [which] was made in 1899"*. Little in the way of photographic or other records exist of the early Humber company, although some correspondence between Humber's head office in Coventry and the said Mr Hicks has been discovered by John Tarring. Whilst this is a direct consequence of there being very few Humber cars being made prior to 1900, one well documented example was a vehicle known as the MD Voiturette at the 1899 Stanley Show. Powered by a 2¼ h.p. De Dion-Bouton engine driving the front wheels, this curious machine was steered by the rear wheels using a steering wheel which could be raised and given a sharp turn to start the engine. In *The Humber Story*, Demaus and Tarring make reference to a car described in the 1903 catalogue as *"an electric car, of which one of our engineers was joint inventor"*. It is thought that this refers to a design by Mr C H Shacklock, an engineer at Humber's Wolverhampton works. Certainly by 1900, conventional De Dion Bouton-based 3 h.p., 3½ h.p. and 5 h.p. models of a conventional design were being produced.

1902 Humber 12 h.p., the first four-cylinder Humber

Curiously, mention is made in the 1901 Humber catalogue that the company *"had found it necessary to ..confine ourselves as far as mechanism is concerned to one standard pattern"* and further, that *"purchasers ..need have no fear of being troubled with litigation for infringement, which at present is an important consideration, having in view the many cases which have recently been fought and which are still pending"*. Clearly, the company was so anxious to distance itself from Pennington and Lawson, that it felt it necessary to advertise this in its sales literature.

Humber's fortunes continued to turn with the recruitment of Louis Coatalen in 1901. Born in Concarneau, France in 1879, Coatalen proved to be a model student who had been selected for a three year full-time course at the Ecole des Arts et Metiers in Paris, after which he worked at the drawing offices of Panhard, then Clement and finally at De Dion-Bouton, from where he was recruited by Charles Crowden of Leamington Spa. Following Crowden's decision not to go into the manufacturing of motor cars, Coatalen moved to Coventry, where he was recruited by the Humber company as chief engineer. With the recruitment of Coatalen in 1901, Humber's motor car designs became comparatively successful, particularly in the 1902 season, which saw the introduction of Coatalen's 12 h.p. design, the show car carrying a limousine body with curved windows of plate glass. The basic chassis, which was powered by a four-cylinder engine (the cylinders being cast in pairs) had electric and tube ignition and a four-speed gearbox. This design continued virtually unaltered into 1903, when it was joined by the larger 20 h.p. model with mechanically operated inlet and exhaust valves on opposite sides of a T-shaped combustion chamber.

5 h.p. Humberette.

6 ½ h.p. Humberette.

1906 10-12 h.p. Coventry Humber.

18

The 1905 Beeston Humber Four-Cylinder Cars.

1905 catalogue cover.

Coatalen's influence also induced Humber to take part in competitive events, for Coatalen saw competitive success as a means of promotion of production cars and increasing sales. Two of the 12 h.p. four-cylinder models were entered for the Automobile Club of Great Britain and Ireland's 650-mile reliability trial in 1902, one driven by H Belcher, an ex-racing cyclist who had been general manager of the Beeston works since 1895. No notable success was achieved at this trial, although a new 20 h.p. Humber of 1903 made some progress at the "Irish Fortnight" speed trials and hill climbs which followed the Gordon Bennett Trophy Race of that year.

Following Belcher's resignation in 1904, his successor, T C Pullinger, embarked on a more active competition policy, with a number of vehicles being specifically designed for racing purposes in an ambitious programme which appears to have been in response to the successes of a Scottish competitor, Arroll-Johnstone, who had won the first Isle of Man Tourist Trophy in 1905.

Coatalen based his 1905 competition cars on the 8/10 h.p., 10/12 h.p. and 16/20 h.p. production cars, basically of touring specification, only just under the weight limit allowed by the TT race rules. None of entrants were very successful. For the 1906 event a 16/20 h.p. Beeston Humber, shorn of excess weight, was driven by Pullinger and a 20 h.p. Coventry Humber was driven by Coatalen, even though the weight of this car was some 600lb over the minimum permissible. Both Humbers performed reasonably well, Pullinger finishing in fifth place and Coatalen in sixth and they achieved overall speeds of 32.6 and 32.1 miles per hour respec-

tively, but some way behind the 39.3 mph achieved by the winning Rolls-Royce.

Whilst the works racing Humbers were comparatively unsuccessful, a number of privately owned vehicles had some success in the sprints and reliability trials of 1905 and 1906. Although not directly involved, the company attached some importance to these trials and made a point of producing a summary of the various competition successes in it's 1907 catalogue.

Meanwhile, the company introduced the 5 h.p. Humberette, the first Humber motor car to be produced in any numbers, a total of 500 being produced by the Beeston and Coventry works in the first six months of 1903. The Beeston cars, capitalising on the idiosyncratic differentiation between the products from these "rival" factories, were more expensive than the Coventry cars, though of virtually identical basic specification. These small single-cylinder cars proved to be relatively popular and were, curiously enough, listed in the firm's motor cycle catalogue rather than the motor car catalogue, possibly to provide a bridge between the cyclist and the motorist.

By 1904, the Humberette was being further refined with a choice of 5 h.p. or 6½ h.p. engines. Although the early success of the Humberette range continued through 1904, it becoming the most popular of British light cars at the time, production was phased out and efforts directed towards larger, well-appointed cars in the following years. With the disappearance of the Humberette range of cars in 1906, the company concentrated on the 10/12 h.p. and Coatalen-designed 16/20 h.p cars. The 16/20 proved to be relatively fast by Edwardian standards, and a 1905 model had been

Humber stand at the 1906 Olympia Motor Show. A 15 h.p. Touring car is on the left, a 10/12 h.p. with hood and screen "for doctor's use" is on the right.

chosen to represent the company at the Tourist Trophy Race in the Isle of Man. Whereas the 10/12 h.p. continued unaltered, the Beeston 16/20 h.p. was enlarged to 30 h.p. and made available in chassis form for £495. A number of Humber-built bodies were offered for prices between £525 and £675, which included a six-seater Landaulette, Limousine or Berline bodies. A new four-cylinder 15 h.p. was added to the range in 1907.

The reasons for this were mainly financial. In 1904, the Humber company made only £1,125 profit despite the popularity of the Humberette. This increased to £6,537 in 1905, but by 1906 when the 10/12 h.p. and 16/20 h.p. were the mainstay of the Humber range, profits soared to £106,559 and production to 1,000 cars. By this time, popularity of the vehicles was such that the chairman was moved to remark that *"we were almost driven to assembling the vehicles in the street, so great did the demand outstrip our factory capacity."*

In Humber's case, optimistic investment in the new works at Humber Road resulted in serious over-capacity, and this, together with tight and non-existent profit margins during 1907, was to bring the firm close to insolvency the following year.

1907 15 h.p. Coventry Humber in Palace Yard, Hereford.

3. Quality And Style Before Performance

1907 proved to be a difficult year for Humber. One of the most serious problems was the departure of Louis Coatalen, who left to join the rival Hillman concern. However, the downturn in car sales in 1907 combined with the substantial over-capacity at the Folly Lane works during 1908 was a far more pressing problem.

With this increasing pressure on space, Humber had put in motion plans for a massive 22-acre works at Folly Lane, Stoke, Coventry (later renamed Humber Road) which would be the largest in the Coventry area. With the opening of the new works, the factory at Beeston would be closed. However, the follow-up to the boom year of 1906 was a downturn in sales, a glut of motor vehicles and a price war amongst the motor manufacturers.

The building of the Folly Lane works had been entrusted to Walter J Phillips, who whilst making remarkable progress in the construction of the costly new factory, soon made it more than obvious that the Humber concern was running out of money. A new share issue in 1907 proved to be a disappointment with only 39,174 of the 100,000 30-Shilling shares offered to the shareholders being allotted by 22 January 1908. 30,413 of the remaining shares were offered at 5-Shillings per share, but this too proved to be a disappointment, and the financial position of the company continued to deteriorate through 1908. Despite the closure of the Wolverhampton works, the company found itself with an increased overhead in a period when sales were plummeting. Talk circulated in Coventry of Humber cars filling back yards and Humber recorded a substantial loss of £23,082 in 1908, with no immediate prospect of a return to profitability.

At a Board meeting held early in 1909, Edward Powell, the managing director, had the uncomfortable task of accounting for the appalling financial situation. The whole of the loss for 1908 was attributed to the motor department in Coventry, who had continued to turn out vehicles at an extraordinary rate, despite falling orders and a general downturn in the trade. This glut of vehicles was difficult enough to dispose of, and, to encourage sales, dealers had then been allowed larger discounts, which in some cases had eliminated what little profit was available. When this state of affairs was communicated to the shareholders, Lord Russell, a wealthy shareholder, moved that a committee be formed to investigate this sorry state of affairs and that it's proposals be presented to an extraordinary general meeting.

Convened in February 1909, the committee presented a damning indictment of the management of the business, and the meeting resolved that the company go into voluntary liquidation and be reconstructed as a new company with the same name. In the event all but one

The engine assembly shop, Humber works, Beeston.

1907 15 h.p. four-cylinder Coventry Humber. Purchased for £600 cash on 18th September, 1907 at the Schumacher Cycle and Motor Agency in Adelaide, by Alfred May. His son, Hedley May, is seen here driving his father and sisters. Hedley recalled that "The Humber had a four-cylinder engine, all cylinders separate to the engine. There was no electrical equipment apart from the magneto, kerosene side and tail lamps and a Lucas acetylene head lamp. Tyre pressure was 90lb and the tyres held on with security bolts. Petrol was fed to the engine by gravity from the tank mounted under the driver's seat."

of the directors resigned, Russell was appointed Chairman, J A Cole Managing Director and H G Burford, formerly of Mercedes and Milnes-Daimler, Works Manager. Further, it was decided to utilise the spare capacity at Folly Lane for the production of aircraft and motor cycles.

Humber offered its own aeroplanes and engines along with Bleriot wings at £440 per pair and propellers for £12.12 shillings "guaranteed perfect". This new undertaking had been entered into upon the initiative of Ballin Hinde, one of the Humber directors. The company at first offered the Bleriot machines to the public, although by 1911 a new Humber bi-plane was offered for sale. However, the aero department failed to live up to its early promise and was closed in 1911.

1908 saw the introduction of a Coventry-built 30 h.p. "six", Humbers first production six-cylinder car and the last of the Beeston produced Humbers prior to the closure of the Beeston factory later in the year. The 1909 model year saw a new 8 h.p. two-cylinder, two-seater car added to the range, together with a new 16 h.p. four-cylinder car with prices ranging from £385 for a standard tonneau to £555 for a six-seater D-front landaulette.

1910 saw little change to the Humber range, apart from offering Humber detachable wheels as standard throughout the range and the option of increasingly popular new wire wheels. New body styles on the 12 h.p. model were offered, including a "racing type" two-seater, priced at £285 and fitted with the racy wire wheels as standard. These wheels appear to have been the fastest feature of the car, which differed little in performance from a more conventional standard-bodied four seater. 12 h.p. models were subject to two price rises in May and August 1910, "owing to increased cost of production" and no doubt to the easing of over-capacity in previous years.

1911 saw two completely new models, a 10/14 h.p. two-seater, four-cylinder car at £295, which could be bought in chassis-only form for £270 and the largest

of the range, a 28 h.p., an imposing four cylinder car with a choice of long and short wheelbase chassis. This year also saw a standardisation of the Humber range, with all models bearing a family resemblance, a trait that was to remain until the 1930s.

The following year, 1912, saw new models listed including a 11 h.p. which was the first Humber to be powered by a four-cylinder monobloc engine. A 14 h.p model was also introduced, and curiously, had a three speed, as opposed to four-speed gearbox. This was the responsibility of Theodore James Biggs, who was originally employed at Humber from 1906 to 1909, had returned in April 1912, and was an important influence in the design of Humber cars in the succeeding years.

This first became evident in 1913 with the modification of the monobloc 11 h.p. car and the introduction of a new 14 h.p. model, both fitted with four-speed gearboxes and detachable wire wheels. The Humberette also made a reappearance, this time as a cyclecar with a V-twin air-cooled engine with live axles and bevel gears. A lively little car by the standards of the time, this two seater sold for £125 and proved to be comparatively popular. 1914 saw one newcomer in the shape of a 10 h.p., which was the basis of a range that was to continue until 1928. This up-to-date small car was offered in two

1907 10/12 h.p. Coventry Humber 4-seater Tourer.

1907 Isle of Man Tourist Trophy TT Race. C H Cooper in a 20/30 h.p. Humber taking part in the heavy touring car race. The race was won over 201 ¼ miles in a time of 7 hours and 11 minutes at an average speed of 28.7 miles per hour.

and four-seater form, with prices ranging from £255 to £270. Meanwhile the Humberette was offered in water-cooled form at £135, and the most expensive and well-appointed 28 h.p. six-seater cabriolet at £650.

In the meantime, Humber's racing programme continued. With a change in the rules of the Isle of Man Tourist Trophy races in 1908, the decision was made to make a radical departure from the design of the company's Beeston entrants of previous years. Overhead camshaft engines replaced the production side-valve units and the body was reduced to the bare minimum required under the rules, consisting of a platform for bolster petrol tank and two bucket seats. The exposed engines were protected by a fine wire mesh cage and quick-detachable, centre-lock wheels were fitted. Despite all these modifications, neither of the two Beeston entrants had much success, nor did the more conventional Coventry entrant, all retiring with mechanical problems.

With the closure of the Beeston works in 1908 and the departure of Pullinger to Arroll-Johnston in 1909, Humber's racing programme was later to come under the management of Biggs, who prepared special 11.9 h.p. and 14 h.p. cars for record breaking and sprints in 1912 and 1913. At the July 1912 flying half mile attempt at Brooklands, Class B records were broken by the 11.9 h.p. car at speeds of 71.62, 71.77 and 70.82 for the flying half-mile, flying kilometer and flying mile respectively. With the 14 h.p. Humber, the same records in Class C were taken at 75.6, 74.44 and 73.32

Following the change in the TT rules, the 1908 Humber entrants were more obviously race-prepared than those from previous years. The chassis was merely a platform for the engines and minimal driver and passenger accommodation. The top photograph is of the Beeston Humber No 18 driven by W G Tuck, the second photo of a Beeston Humber driven by James Ried and the photo immediately above is the Coventry Humber.

Behind the group can be seen a 1910 25 h.p. Humber Bleriot-type Monoplane.

1910 16 h.p. Touring car for Earl Radnor.

1910 12 h.p. 4 seated Landaulette catalogue illustration.

respectively and a 2024cc rebored 11.9 h.p. car broke further Class B 10-lap records in May 1913 with a speed of 76.45 mph. By October 1913, Humber was able to announce that a Humber car driven by W G Tuck held every record in Class B. Tuck enjoyed a number of hill-climb and sprint successes, particularly at the Saltburn speed trials and Shelsley Walsh hill-climbs.

In 1913, Tuck took a first and second place at the Easter meeting at Brooklands, and a first and third place at the Brooklands bank-holiday meeting in 1914 driving his 20 h.p. TT Humber, shortly after the Isle of Man TT races.

For the 1914 TT races, Frederick T Burgess, Humber's designer, had produced a team of three cars with 3295cc engines. These cars were remarkably expensive to build, costing some £15,000 in total and they closely resembled the 1913 Coupe de l'Auto Peugeots in having 16-valve, twin-cam, four-cylinder engines, but differed in having the exhausts on the driver's side rather than the mechanics.

No identification ascribed these cars as Humbers and one went to Bentley's in 1919, Burgess having joined W O Bentley at this time. Burgess drove one of these Humbers in the two-day 600-mile TT, the others

being driven by Sam Wright and W G Tuck. Burgess' car retired with a seized piston, and Tuck and Wright retired on the first and second day, both with valve trouble.

With the outbreak of war in 1914, car production continued, albeit with a number of changes. The larger models were discontinued and production concentrated on the 10 h.p., 11 h.p. and 14 h.p. models The air-cooled Humberette was dropped. Wartime models included delivery vans on the 10 h.p. and 11 h.p. models and an ambulance body on the 14 h.p.

Surprisingly, given Humber's previous experience in aircraft manufacture, they did not immediately become involved in wartime aircraft production. However, after a change in policy, Humber manufactured a number of aircraft, including the Avro 504, the Avro 504K, 320 h.p. "Dragonfly" engines and W O Bentley's BR rotary aeroplane engines.

With the cessation of hostilities, Lt Col. J A Cole, who had originally joined the Humber board as managing director, was made chairman in 1919. A motorist since 1898, Cole had been chairman of the Lincolnshire Automobile Club and vice-president of the Motor Union. Although he had an engineering background, Cole's views on motor vehicle design practice were

1910 16 h.p. Humber.

1914 11 h.p. two-seater catalogue illustration.

clutches as late as 1928 and Humbers were not even to be fitted with front wheel brakes until 1925, some two years after their competitors because Cole regarded them as a *"costly and possibly dangerous mechanism"*.

A number of detailed modifications were made to the Humber "Ten", but the "Fourteen" was the first of Humber's models to be significantly modified with a new 15.9 h.p. engine with increased bore and a lengthened wheelbase. This larger chassis provided the basis for some beautifully made bodies, the standard offerings being a large five-seater tourer and a tall, imposing saloon. Curiously, these cars were marketed as owner-driver's cars with no division for a chauffeur, very unusual for such an expensive car, priced at £750 for a tourer and £1,010 for the saloon.

However, by 1921, the Humber range, especially the "Ten" was beginning to look somewhat dated, having more in common with 1914 cars than its contemporaries, so a number of revisions, rather than outright modifications, were made. The two-seater cars were now available as 2-3 seaters and the engine was bored out to give a rating of 11.4 h.p. The body was revised to give it a "family" resemblance to the 15.9 h.p. car, with a higher radiator and bonnet line, and modifications to the wings and body contours. Despite the modifications to the engine the model continued to be marketed as the "Ten" until 1922, when its official designation was changed to the 11.4 h.p. Further styling changes were made in 1922 with the introduction of a new single-door saloon.

The 1923 season saw the most significant change in the Humber range of the decade, the decision to adopt inlet-over-exhaust valves. This was to be a feature of all Humber models until 1932, when the Rootes rationalization of production resulted in the changeover to side valves for the 1933 season models. The same year, an

conservative even by the standards of the day, and his influence was to dominate the Humber range of vehicles until the late 1920s when the Rootes brothers were to effectively take over the Humber concern as part of their ambitious plan to create a British manufacturing combine along the lines of the American General Motors.

Following the end of the First World War, Humber resumed production of two of its pre-war models, the "Ten" and the "Fourteen". With the return of servicemen, and the growth of the motor vehicle as a utility and leisure vehicle, the demand for motor cars in the immediate post-war years cushioned many firms from the need to make long term plans for the development of a new range of cars and to modernise design and production methods.

Humber was perhaps the most extreme example of the conservative approach to design prevailing at the time. Whilst Humber under Edward Powell may have taken a different path, Cole's policies retained such Edwardian features as separate gearboxes and cone

1914-15 Humber 14 h.p. Tourer Trailer Ambulance presented to BRCS by the employees of the Humber sawmill.

Aircraft Inspectorate staff are pictured here in front of the Humber built BR-2 engines designed by W O Bentley. The aircraft they were fitted in, the Avro 504 biplane, is shown on the right, both photos date from March 1919.

The Humber 14 h.p. The examples here, dating from 1919, were Police cars.

all-new small car was introduced, the Humber Light Car, or 8 h.p., a lively model, which was refined and well equipped compared to other light cars and cyclecars, though far more expensive. The first models were bodied with the single-shell "chummy", designed to seat three adults or two adults and two children. These were joined in 1924 by a miniature saloon and a two/three seater with dickey seat. The "Chummy" and two/three seater were priced at £250 and the saloon at £310, pricier than comparative models such as the Austin Seven.

This range of Humbers was well liked and well built. In the March 1st 1944 edition of *The Motor*, a retrospective of the Humber 15.9 h.p. was carried out.

"..the 15.9 h.p. Humber carried on the pre-war tradition of touring in comfort, and was designed particularly to appeal to the growing number of owner-drivers in layout, performance and equipment. The last-named particularly was extremely full, and, when such refinements were often listed as extras, the Humber was sold complete with starter, speedometer, petrol gauge, electric horn, spare wheel, jack, clock, hood, and side curtains on the tourer: whilst the saloon had adjustable driver's seat, hand operated windscreen wiper, roof lights, paper and parcels rack, ash trays, spring-loaded windows and roof ventilators....

"In performance the car was very well suited to its public. Unlike some of its high geared contemporar-

1920 10 h.p. 2/3 seated Humber. This particular example was the company's Motor Show car.

A second Humber show car from 1920. This example is a 15.9 h.p. Tourer.

26

1920 photograph of a selection the Humber range of cars.

A rather attractive 1921 10 h.p. Coupe.

1922. The Humber West End showroom. The cars are 11.4 h.p. 2-seaters, tourers and a saloon.

The Humber office block at Humber Road Coventry, with a selection of the company's range from 1922. 11.4 h.p. Tourers, a coupe and a four-seater are pictured here. Note the family resemblence which characterised the Humber range of the 1920s

1927 Humber 9/20 Tourer.

1927 Humber 12/25 Tourer without front wheel brakes.

ies, it would run down to a fast walking pace in top as well as up to 60 (mph) downhill. It handled well, the steering was light and it was not often called off top gear by main road hills....

"For a car of its size, the petrol consumption of between 20 and 25 m.p.g. was remarkably good, particularly in view of the roomy and luxurious coach work fitted....the 15.9 was deservedly popular..."

For 1925, Humber continued to make detailed improvements to it's range, with the 11.4 h.p. being bored out to 1795cc and being redesignated the 12/25. The rest of the range was similarly renamed 8/18 and 15/40 respectively, the second figure being an approximation of brake horsepower. The main technical development of that year was the fitting of front wheel brakes to the 15/40 as an option, though grudgingly, and in such a way that minimal braking power was applied to the front wheels. There was a view at the time that the fitting of efficient braking systems deterred careful

driving a view vigourously endorsed by Col. Cole.

1926 was the last year of production for the 12/25, but development of the 15/40 continued with optional front wheel brakes now becoming standard. The most significant change to the Humber range was to the appearance of the bodywork, with four doors now becoming standard on the tourer saloon and landaulette. The smallest car in the range was the popular 9/20, an enlarged version of the 8/18, bore being increased to give a capacity of 1056cc and the wheelbase being extended from 7ft 10½ in to 8ft 6in and the track being widened, and the overall appearance of the car was that of a "miniature" of the larger Humbers, which no doubt contributed to the popularity of this model. That year saw the announcement of an all-new model, the six-cylinder (the first since before the First World War) Humber 20/55, which appeared in July 1926, in time for the 1927 season. Though conservative in engineering, this 3075cc was offered as a large five-seater tourer, a saloon, limousine or landaulette.

This was followed by a replacement for the 12/25, a "four", derived from the "six", an idiosyncratic development which was contrary to the more usual practice of developing a four and adding two pots to make a six. The 2050cc 14/40 was a popular car which was more imposing than its predecessor, but in the same price range, £460 purchased an open car and £575 an attractive ¾ coupe or a saloon. With superior all weather equipment, these were the most comfortable production (rather than coachbuilt) car of the 1920s. With this new range a total of 2,507 cars were produced in 1927, 1,266 being the new 14/40 model. All had a "family" appearance making them instantly recognisable, and were widely recognised as fine luxury cars. This recognition attracted the attentions of the ambitious Rootes brothers.

4. THE ROOTES TAKEOVER

William Edward Rootes and Reginald Claude Rootes were born in Hawkhurst, Kent in 1894 and 1896 respectfully. The sons of William Rootes, a cycle shop proprietor, they were educated at Cranbrook school, while the elder Rootes developed his business in a motor car agency, selling Ford, Morris, Wolseley, Itala, Humber, Singer and Sunbeam cars. "Billy" Rootes joined Singer Motors in 1909, serving his apprenticeship before returning to run a new branch of the family business in Maidstone in 1913. Reginald, meanwhile, trained as an accountant and entered the civil service.

Following the end of the First World War, the brothers were each presented with a cheque for £1,200 by their father, with which they formed *Rootes Limited*. Billy Rootes' talents as a salesman and Reginald's training as an administrator were a powerful combination. Surviving the slump of the early 1920s they then formed Rootes Distributors, with showrooms in Long Acre and Bond Street, London, from where they distributed Austin cars in London and the Home Counties. Austin itself was expanding rapidly at the time, and Rootes Distributors prospered on the back of this expansion in the mid 1920s.

By 1924 a stake had been taken in the Birmingham garage chain of George Heath, and in 1925 Rootes took over *Thrupp & Maberly*, the London coachbuilding firm. Behind this flurry of corporate activity the Rootes brothers had formulated a long-term strategy of controlling a manufacturing combine, a chain of distributors and coachbuilders. In this, they were remarkably advanced in their thinking, preferring to build up the Rootes empire by the acquisition of established names rather than by organic growth. Their timing in the 1920s was excellent, since many firms that had prospered in the early period of the motor industry were now facing the economic realities of a mass market which was subject to the ebb and flow of boom and recession. In the 1920s, there were many opportunities for an acquisition-hungry group, particularly amongst those companies who had good reputations but were in a parlous financial state.

The Rootes brother's strengths lay not in their engineering expertise, but in their sales and marketing acumen combined with financial flair. These qualities were essential as the motor industry became more sophisticated, and it was the Rootes emphasis on management, with engineering talent "bought in" which accounts for their remarkable growth from a distributorship to a manufacturing combine in such a short time.

With the move to Devonshire House, Piccadilly in 1926 there was some concern that the Rootes empire was overreaching itself, which was not helped by the abortive investment in Reginald Maudslay's Standard company in the early 1920s, nor by an abortive takeover bid for Clyno in 1927, and a second attempt to mount a bid for the Standard company. However, having taken stakes in the private Hillman and public Humber concerns in the late 1920s an opportunity arose for a bid when both companies began negotiations for a projected merger which would, it was hoped, solve both their respective problems. By this time the Rootes brothers had persuaded Sir George E (later Lord) May to provide the backing of a substantial institutional investor, the Prudential Assurance Company. With the acquisition of minority stakes in both Hillman and Humber in 1927 and 1928, and the acquisition of the Midland bank shares by the Prudential in 1930, the influence of the Rootes brothers was soon felt at board level, evidenced by Humber's decision to sell its cycle business to Raleigh and to close down it's motor cycle operation in order to concentrate on motor vehicle manufacture, particularly following the acquisition of the commercial vehicle concern, Commer, in November 1926.

However, this failed to have the desired effect on the Humber company's fortunes. Like many other companies in the late 1920s Humber had failed to address the problem of outdated plant and production methods and by 1927 the company had manufactured only 2,507 cars in the year, and in 1928, for the first time since 1917, failed to pay its shareholders a dividend when a trading loss of £36,806 was announced. This was partly attributable to a general malaise in the market, where demand for the up-market Humbers was falling, but the increasing production costs of these old-fashioned cars was a significant factor.

Hillman was in a similar position, with a board dominated by the ailing William Hillman and John Black. Negotiations between Cole and Hillman continued through 1928 with a merger being announced late

Humber 14/40 with Coupe body by Bridges Garage, Cirencester.

1928 Humber 20/55 5/7 seater Landaulette.

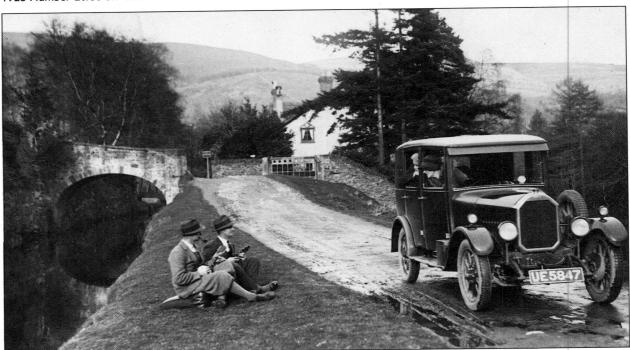

1928 Humber 9/20 Fabric Saloon.

in the December of that year, when Humber's share capital was increased to finance the cost of the merger, which progressively increased through the 1929 financial year when the company lost some £67,158. This unfortunate combination left the Humber company with severe cash flow problems, even though the proposed merger was to *"..achieve economies of scale, general administration and production methods"*, according to the press release.

With the company experiencing large losses, no new Humber models were announced in 1928, though in common with many luxury car manufacturers, Humber offered a choice of fabric-bodied saloons, and made minor modifications to bodywork, as well as dispensing with the "trough and splash" lubrication system and replacing the ludicrously old-fashioned cone clutches

with a single plate clutch. 1929 was the year when several confident announcements of new models were made. A medium "six", the 16/50 was an all-new model, although the 14/40 was still listed at reduced prices. Powered by a new 2110cc engine, a number of new features were introduced, such as brake lights incorporated in the tail lamp, Bendix-Perrot four-wheel brakes and a new and taller radiator and grille, giving the car a slightly more modern appearance. Several body styles were offered, a four-light Weymann fabric-finished saloon, a tourer, a coachbuilt six-light saloon and a fabric-bodied Sportsman's coupe. The 9/26 was redesignated the 9/28 and the 20/55 redesignated 20/65, both models having had revisions to increase power output, the 20/65 Snipe featuring a 3075cc inlet over exhaust valve arrangement for the six-cylinder engine.

1931 Humber Snipe 20/70.

Several changes were made to the appearance of the 9/28. The merger with Hillman had resulted from the juxtaposition of the two factories in Coventry, and whilst it was announced in *The Autocar* that each marque would continue to bear separate identities, a telling phrase in an Autocar article noted that the combine's export activities would be managed by Rootes. Despite the rhetoric about separate identities, these Hillman and Humber cars were remarkably similar in appearance.

Production for Humber in 1929 was up on the previous year, despite the effects of the Wall Street

crash, and with the influence of the Rootes brothers beginning to be felt, a number of changes were made to the management of the group. Although no significant changes were made to the vehicles, changes in policy and personnel were introduced. Humber motor cycle production was finally phased out in 1930. A number of key appointments were made, Captain John Irving, who had designed three land speed record cars, including the Golden Arrow, a Thrupp & Maberly-bodied special car driven by Sir Henry Segrave. Irving joined in autumn 1929 as technical chief and Alfred Wilde was poached from Standard to join Irving, whose management style was less abrasive than John Black's. Irving's first task was to design a new car with which the Rootes brothers intended to compete on equal terms with the American Chryslers and Buicks, and Irving presented a Humber "Snipe", a car with clear transatlantic styling influences which was combined with Humber's engine technology. In this he was assisted by William Heynes who had joined Humber as an apprentice in 1922, and was by then in charge of the technical department. Heynes was later to leave the Rootes group to join SS Cars, and was one of the engineers responsible for the Jaguar XK engine and the Jaguar racing cars of the 1950s.

Investment was made in new manufacturing facilities at Humber Road with the erection of new buildings to the south of the site to accommodate new machinery, which resulted in increased production to levels of some 200 cars per week in Spring 1930. By then production methods were beginning to change, with some components being machine assembled, with much of the assembly being completed on a conveyor line. Some 300 bodies would be assembled at any one time, including special orders such as saloon landaulettes with the special trim and fittings. With the installation of £700,000-worth of new machine tools in 1931 and the unification of the two neighbouring Humber and Hillman factories the same year, production capacity was in-

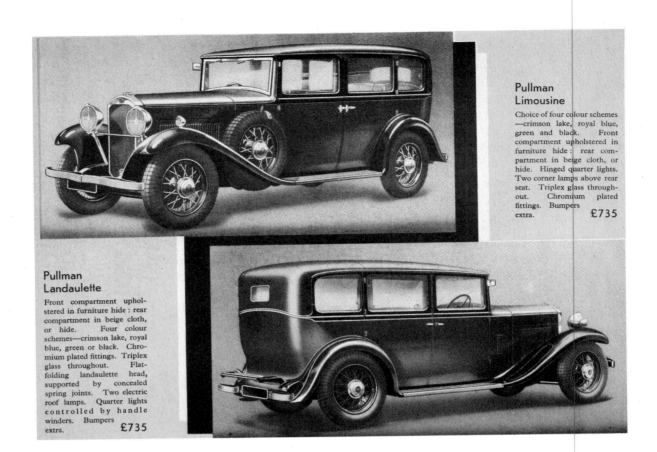

Pullman Limousine

Choice of four colour schemes —crimson lake, royal blue, green and black. Front compartment upholstered in furniture hide : rear compartment in beige cloth, or hide. Hinged quarter lights. Two corner lamps above rear seat. Triplex glass throughout. Chromium plated fittings. Bumpers extra. £735

Pullman Landaulette

Front compartment upholstered in furniture hide : rear compartment in beige cloth, or hide. Four colour schemes—crimson lake, royal blue, green or black. Chromium plated fittings. Triplex glass throughout. Flat-folding landaulette head, supported by concealed spring joints. Two electric roof lamps. Quarter lights controlled by handle winders. Bumpers extra. £735

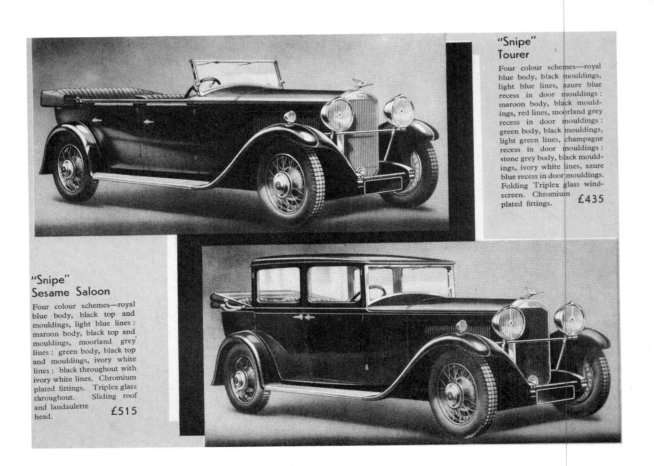

"Snipe" Tourer

Four colour schemes—royal blue body, black mouldings, light blue lines, azure blue recess in door mouldings : maroon body, black mouldings, red lines, moorland grey recess in door mouldings : green body, black mouldings, light green lines, champagne recess in door mouldings : stone grey body, black mouldings, ivory white lines, azure blue recess in door mouldings. Folding Triplex glass windscreen. Chromium plated fittings. £435

"Snipe" Sesame Saloon

Four colour schemes—royal blue body, black top and mouldings, light blue lines : maroon body, black top and mouldings, moorland grey lines : green body, black top and mouldings, ivory white lines : black throughout with ivory white lines. Chromium plated fittings. Triplex glass throughout. Sliding roof and landaulette head. £515

1932 catalogue pictures of the Humber range

1932 Humber Snipe with "Gills" all-weather body.

creased to 100 cars per day, 25,000 cars per year. Nevertheless, the Humber company continued to record substantial losses in 1931 of £96,156, particularly disappointing after profits of £42,275 in 1930. At the annual general meeting, Colonel Cole described 1931 as the blackest year ever. Humber, he claimed, was in better shape than Hillman or Commer, and had increased exports, but finances were tight as *"the world had become seriously impoverished"*, despite talk that Humber-Hillman were to become the British "General Motors" by taking over two other Coventry firms, but this was pure speculation at that time.

Rootes Limited had acquired a substantial stake in the enlarged Humber, becoming a majority shareholder in July 1932, when their stake was built up to 60% via a scheme of arrangement which involved the acquisition of deferred ordinary shares held by the Prudential, Rootes backers and possibly Rootes nominees. Rootes influence over the management had increased in the previous two years, determining the strategy of the company and influencing all major investment decisions.

William and Reginald Rootes became directors of Humber Limited on 10th August 1932. Whilst Colonel Cole remained chairman (an office which he kept until 1943), Billy Rootes was appointed deputy chairman and Reginald Rootes as managing director. Their arrival in the Midlands motoring concern *"caused about as much commotion as the introduction of a fox into a chicken coop"* and the brothers set about turning round the ailing Humber and Hillman companies. However, the company continued to make substantial losses into 1932 of £107,840, although with the gradual reorganisation of the combine and the rationalization of the range of Humber and Hillman cars this loss was to be turned into a £241,886 surplus within four years.

With plans for unheard-of increases in the production of Humber and Hillman cars, one of the most difficult problems was body panels. The old Humbers had been practically hand-built, but this was too slow and expensive for the revitalised Humber, which required a limited number of standard bodies which could be adapted to customer requirements. The one suitable firm for this job was *The Pressed Steel Company of Great Britain Limited,* in which William Morris had had an interest in the 1920s. Humber (and the other Rootes companies) were one of the largest of Pressed Steel's customers in the 1930s, who named their factory exten-

The 1933 Humber Vogue. Built by Humber, this attractive bodystyle was designed in conjunction with Captain Molyneux of Paris, the famous fashion designer of the early 1930s.

1933 Humber Twelve, the body is by a local Australian coachbuilder, although the result was very similar to the factory-built saloon.

Humber Twelve Tourer, one of several bodystyles available on this chassis.

sion after the Rootes brothers, which was commissioned because of need for further production facilities, output having risen sevenfold through the 1930s.

For the more well-heeled, Thrupp & Maberly coachwork was to become a feature of the larger, well-appointed Humbers of the 1930s. The oldest concern to be bought by Rootes, it was founded in 1760 when Joseph Thrupp set up business in George Street, Portman Square, London. Within two years he was commissioned to build a state coach for the Prince of Wales. Joseph Thrupp was succeeded by his son and by 1858 the firm had become known as Charles Thrupp & Company. After eighty years the firm moved to Oxford Street and in 1858 a partnership was formed

the external appearance of the car (as will seen from this illustration) is extremely l proportioned and very pleasing.

direction indicators automatically t up as they are raised and fold y flush when not in use.

Performance that will surprise even the staunchest Humber admirer . . . in this handsome new HUMBER 16/60 Six-light Saloon · £435

Rear view showing hinged quarter lig luggage grid and the graceful sweep the rear panel over the petrol tank ap

luxuriously finished rear compart-t showing the folding tables, centre est, companion sets, etc.

This patented drop-glass partition be fitted to the 16/60 6-light Saloon on an extra charge of £30.

Nothing could be neater than the f board and controls. The wiper motor entirely concealed in the panel. (Note i

between the Thrupp concern and George Maberly of Welbeck Street and Marylebone Lane. By the 1890s, the firm was building bodies for motor vehicles and absorbed many rival coachbuilding firms such as Keens, Rogers, Holmes Brothers, Holland and Holland, Wyburn and Company and Silk and Sons. In 1924, they moved to larger premises in Cricklewood and were bought by Rootes the following year.

Production of all-new Humber models under the Rootes regime was delayed for two years, and Humber continued to manufacture cars which were developments of those offered prior to the Rootes takeover. Change in the company's strategy can be seen with the concentration on the medium to larger cars and disposal of the cycle and motor cycle businesses. This redirection resulted in an increase in production and the introduction of the much revised 16/50 and the John Irving designed Humber "Snipe". The smaller cars were phased out by 1931, the Nines after a production run of only 1,248.

The Humber Snipe was powered by a six-cylinder 25/70 i.o.e. 3498.5cc engine, which was derived from the 20/65 unit. Replacement of the Zenith carburettors with Stromberg UX3s improved petrol consumption to 18-20 m.p.g. and the old Autovac was now replaced with an AC mechanical pump. New arrangements were made with the gearbox, which for the first time was bolted up to the crankcase as a "unit" and had constant mesh helical gears. These gears were quieter under load, but the driver still had to double de-clutch to synchronize gears before changing. The hand retard/ advance to the distributor was still retained, but the unit was comparatively powerful, producing 70 b.h.p., compared with the 50 b.h.p. produced by most other engines of similar size at the time. Several attractive bodystyles were offered, a tourer, drop-head coupe, six-light Weymann saloon and a four-door Weymann coupe. A longer wheelbase chassis was offered, the Humber Pullman, which provided the basis for elaborate coachwork by Thrupp & Maberly, the "cabriolette" de-ville, at £1,095. However the more modest Snipe was priced at £410 in chassis form, compared with £495 for the Pullman chassis, with prices ranging from £495 to

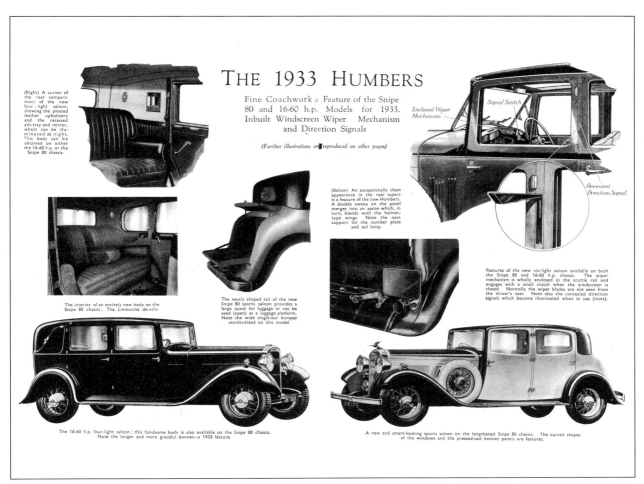

THE 1933 HUMBERS

Fine Coachwork a Feature of the Snipe 80 and 16-60 h.p. Models for 1933. Inbuilt Windscreen Wiper Mechanism and Direction Signals

(Further illustrations are reproduced on other pages)

(Right) A corner of the rear compartment of the new four-light saloon, showing the pleated leather upholstery and the recessed ash-tray and mirror, which can be illuminated at night. This body can be obtained on either the 16-60 h.p. or the Snipe 80 chassis.

Signal Switch

Enclosed Wiper Mechanism

Recessed Direction Signal

(Below) An exceptionally clean appearance in the rear aspect is a feature of the new Humbers. A double sweep on the panel merges into an apron which, in turn, blends with the helmet-type wings. Note the neat support for the number plate and tail lamp.

The interior of an entirely new body on the Snipe 80 chassis: The Limousine de-ville.

The neatly shaped tail of the new Snipe 80 sports saloon provides a large space for luggage or can be used (open) as a luggage platform. Note the wide single-bar bumper standardized on this model.

Features of the new six-light saloon available on both the Snipe 80 and 16-60 h.p. chassis. The wiper mechanism is wholly enclosed in the scuttle rail and engages with a small clutch when the windscreen is closed. Normally the wiper blades are not seen from the driver's seat. Note also the concealed direction signals which become illuminated when in use (inset).

The 16-60 h.p. four-light saloon; this handsome body is also available on the Snipe 80 chassis. Note the longer and more graceful bonnet—a 1933 feature.

A new and smart-looking sports saloon on the lengthened Snipe 80 chassis. The curved shapes of the windows and the pressed-out bonnet panels are features.

The 1933 Humber programme, with contemporary shots of detailed changes.

£565 for the various Snipe bodystyles. The Humber Snipe of this year was the first to carry the famous snipe radiator mascot.

The Humber 16/50 was virtually identical to the Snipe in appearance, though less powerful. The 16/50 "Imperial" was the cheapest of this range priced at £410 for a tourer and £435 for the saloon, but this base model was stripped of many of the refinements of the other models and distinguished by old-fashioned steel artillery wheels. The 1931 16/50 Humber Saloon was described in the April 3rd 1931 edition of *The Autocar* as:

"Well thought out in all its details, this 1931 model 16 h. p. half panelled Weymann saloon proves under test to be attractive from many points of view. The size of the car and its capabilities make it peculiarly suitable to the needs of the modern household, for either town work or for touring in the hands of any driver. It has a good all-round performance and is particularly easy to handle."

The Autocar concluded that:

"..the 16 h.p. Humber is a very attractive kind of car, well found in all it's details, well thought out, practical, very comfortable, convenient and good to look at."

Rootes' main efforts were concentrated on the launch of the Hillman Wizard and the Hillman Minx in 1931, and the first completely new Humber car under the new regime was the Humber 12 HP in 1932. By this time

1934 advertisement for the Humber Twelve, just prior to the restyling of the radiator grille.

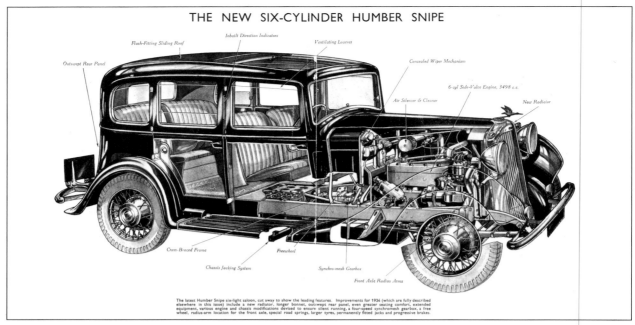

THE NEW SIX-CYLINDER HUMBER SNIPE

Flush-Fitting Sliding Roof

Inbuilt Direction Indicators

Ventilating Louvres

Outswept Rear Panel

Concealed Wiper Mechanism

6-cyl Side-Valve Engine, 3498 c.c.

Air Silencer & Cleaner

New Radiator

Cross-Braced Frame

Freewheel

Chassis Jacking System

Synchro-mesh Gearbox

Front Axle Radius Arms

The latest Humber Snipe six-light saloon, cut away to show the leading features. Improvements for 1934 (which are fully described elsewhere in this issue) include a new radiator, longer bonnet, outswept rear panel, even greater seating comfort, extended equipment, various engine and chassis modifications devised to ensure silent running, a four-speed synchromesh gearbox, a free wheel, radius-arm location for the front axle, special road springs, larger tyres, permanently fitted jacks and progressive brakes.

1934 season Humber Snipe, as publicised in The Motor in this fine cutaway drawing.

"The Humber Snipe is probably the best known motor mascot in the world. It's protruding beak, which is such a feature of the bird is, in the case of the mascot, made of rubber and therefore deprived of any danger it might otherwise possess." Rootes publicity.

1935 Humber Snipe.

the Rootes strategy for Humber was becoming clearer. Whereas most British manufacturers enjoyed some success as motoring became more popular during the 1930s, the Rootes brothers were perhaps the most successful in finding and exploiting market niches for their cars. Model policy was that Hillman cars would provide for the mass market with prices starting at £163 for the Hillman Minx. Humber, however, would cater for the more rigidly stratified upper and middle classes. This was an important factor. The 1930s social stratum had growing professional classes, where much importance was attached to social status. More than in modern times, social status was determined by an individual's manner and possessions. The Rootes influence on Humber's model policy clearly emerges with the 1930 model year with the Humber Snipe, Humber Pullman, Humber 16/50 and Humber 16/50 "Imperial". Exclusivity was preserved by offering well appointed coachbuilt bodies, which was a continuing feature until the demise of the marque.

Several clear indicators are given about the Rootes marketing technique. Cars were given a clear identity with the use of model names, rather than numerical designations. The Humbers built under Colonel Cole's management in the 1920s were fine vehicles, but the use of a model designation which had a vague relationship to the horsepower rating was unimaginative. "Snipe", "Pullman" and "Imperial" were names that captured the public imagination during a period of deep economic gloom. *The Autocar* of August 21st 1931, reviewing the Humber range of that year said:

"About the new Pullman there is such an aristocratic air, and such a dignified appearance, that the price comes as a surprise, for a large seven seater limousine landaulette, finished as Humber know how to finish a car, inside and out, cannot be called expensive at £735."

This strategy worked. Sales rose from 1,480 in 1930 to 1,593 in 1931. Rootes also concentrated on export markets, their success in this area is demonstrated by the dramatic rise in the proportion of sales to overseas customers from 4% in 1930 to 16% in 1931. Rootes established a number of resident agencies overseas, in India, South Africa, the Far East, Australia and in South America, where the associated company of Rootes Argentina operated from Buenos Aires. This chain was carefully built up from the mid-1920s with a

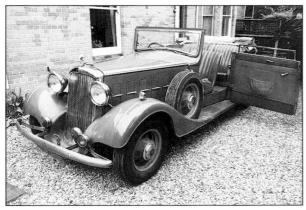

1934 Humber Snipe 80 Foursome Drophead Coupe. This car is in original condition and is shown here as found in 1988.

1935 Humber Twelve saloon, with revised grille. This example was owned by the Earl of Cardigan.

1934 Humber Snipe 80. This example has coachwork by Tickford which featured a full-length wind-down hood.

strong emphasis on sales and service. In particular, the use of autonomous parts distribution points gave the group a much needed lead over it's competitors, when most were specially shipping individual parts overseas to order from bases in England, which usually resulted in customers being unable to use their vehicles for up to three months.

Another point, which comes across in *The Autocar* quote (above) is that Rootes played on the inherent goodwill in the Humber name. The "old" Humber advertising had been factual and extremely conservative in it's approach.

Rootes used model names to great effect. They even named engines and suspension systems. These names may have had little relation to the hardware, but their novelty captured the public's attention which was then retained by the adman's prose, which deliberately played on the social aspirations of the potential owner.

A brief comparison illustrates the difference; the first extract is from an advertisement for the 10 h.p. Humber, the second for a Humber 16/50 from 1931:

"To the owner driver. The 10 h.p. Humber makes a strong appeal. Light yet sturdy: speedy, comfortable, and completely equipped for the road, including electric lighting set and self starter. It's freedom from complications makes it essentially the car for

the owner driver. Here is an interesting letter from one Humber owner who does not employ a driver:

"You will be interested to know that I am just having my 14 h.p. Humber overhauled for the first time. It has done 40,000 miles without a chauffeur or anybody to attend to it and has been on the road every day, seven days a week for practically the whole of the five years. I think this must be very nearly a record, even for a Humber"

By 1933, the Humber advertising had changed both in style and presentation:

"He's out of town on business..."

"He is a director whose voice at a conference can do more good in two hours than a week of negotiating by letter. The man whose work-a-day week finds him in the Potteries on Tuesday, the woollen towns on Wednesday, with business requiring his presence in Bristol and Plymouth before the weekend. He can't wait to "fit in" trains. He drives a car and he drives it hard. Miles to him mean so many minutes. He asks much of his car but thinks little of it. Only that it must be ready for duty day after day without fuss or failure.

"He drives a Humber 16/60. He has owned four of them. He knows they will never let him down"

1932 was an unusually poor year for all motor manufacturers. Humber's production of Snipes, for

Note the clutch between gear box and engine.

Above: Autocar diagram of the De Normanville epicyclic gearbox.
Left: 1935 advertisement featuring a Humber 16/60, with bodywork by Humber. The 16/60 was easily distinguished by the absence of the Snipe mascot on the radiator grille.

Above: 1934 Humber Pullman. This was supplied to a disabled owner, hence the wheelchair arrangement in the rear compartment.
Left: 1935 Humber 16/60 with Carlton Drophead Coupe coachwork.

example, fell from around 1,277 in 1931 to only around 800 in 1932. However, the number of cars exported was encouraging, with the percentage rising from 16% in 1931 to 33% in 1932. With the possibility of recovery in 1933, "new" models were required to take advantage in the anticipated upturn in the economy. Part of this involved the redesign of the Humber Snipe engine. The existing crankcase, sump and crankshaft were retained, but bolted on top was a new cylinder block with side valves. The side-valve engines were able to operate under higher compression ratios and run more efficiently on improved petrol which was appearing at this time. With fewer parts to be manufactured and serviced, production costs were also reduced and the engine continued, albeit with few changes until the 1936 season. This marked the end of the inlet-over-exhaust valve cylinder head arrangement in Humber vehicles.

In 1932, a development of the Humber 16/50 resulted in the introduction of the Humber 16/60 and the Snipe 80 and long-wheelbase "Pullman" for the 1933 season. The 16/60 was virtually a new car, with a new chassis frame with a 10ft 4in wheelbase boxed-in side members alongside the engine and the use of an enlarged bore side-valve Hillman Wizard type engine of 2276cc with a cast-iron combined block and crankcase. Capitalising on the up-market image that Rootes were developing for the marque, the 1932 16/60 brochure stated that:

"The Snipe 80 engine is of higher horsepower than the 16/60, the gear ratios are higher and the tyres are bigger, otherwise the two chassis are identical... in upholstery and equipment all these models are very richly endowed."

The Snipe 80 used a modified overhead-valve development of the old 3498cc Humber 25/70 engine which developed 77 b.h.p. at 3400 r.p.m. Mechanical refinements included silent-third gearboxes, double acting hydraulic dampers and downdraught carburettors. The engine was fitted with a larger capacity water pump and the gearbox with a revised clutch. There was a wide range of bodies, an open tourer, a six-light saloon, a four-light saloon with division and Sesame saloons. Coachbuilt bodies were also offered with a particularly smart foursome coupe by Thrupp & Maberly. All saloons now included Triplex glass and sliding roofs and a left-hand gearchange, in contrast to previous practice, and, by 1933, some of the models offered concealed trafficator and bottom-hinged wipers.

The Pullman chassis generally resembled the Snipe, but with a longer wheelbase. The coachwork offered included a limousine, a landaulette, a limousine de ville and a sports cabriolet de ville by Thrupp & Maberly.

A particularly handsome example in the range was the Humber Snipe "80" Sports Saloon. Reviewed by W G Aston in *Modern Motoring*, the Rootes "house" magazine, in June 1933, this car catered for the social and sporting aspirations of its owners by being both reasonably fast and refined by the day's standards.

".. there never was a happier car - it is also agreeably light to the touch. The steering is beautifully responsive at all speeds: up and down gear changes can be quickly made with the very minimum of effort-and the amount of skill required is almost

negligible - and the action of the pedals is so light that long distances can be carried fast, ithout fatigue.

"Another way in which the striking design differs from most, if not all, of the "developed" models is that not only is it a joy to drive, but it is most charming to ride in.....

"...one quickly sees that the high performance need not necessarily involve discomfort nor any sacrifice of grace and dignity in appearance. The car as a whole is something that the British automobile industry can be proud of."

In 1932, preparations for the 1933 season had seen the introduction of an entirely new four-cylinder model, the Humber Twelve, which sold for £265 in saloon form. Although powered by a relatively small side-valve engine, a 11.98 HP unit of 1669cc, this car had a respectable wheelbase of some 8ft 2in, a track of 4ft 3in and a four forward-speed gearbox with "silent third". Although of modest overall dimensions, interior room was quite generous, enabling four adults to travel in comfort with adequate leg, head and elbow room and rear passengers were provided with foot-rests. Externally the body was shapely and well-proportioned, set off with the new vertical radiator grille. Although a relatively small saloon, Humber emphasised it's "big-car" virtues and it sold well.

For 1934, extensive changes were made to the Humber range of six-cylinder cars. This affected the appearance of the cars and their mechanical specification. The most important mechanical innovation was the introduction of a new four speed gearbox with a single plate clutch, synchromesh in third and top and a free-wheel mounted behind the gearbox casing. Other changes included a modified springing system, redesigned brakes and a jacking system incorporated in the chassis. Externally the new radiator grille design now included new radiator shutters, redesigned wings and a longer bonnet. The radiator shutters were now both thermostatically controlled and operated by oil pressure. This enabled the shutters to close automatically as soon as the engine was stopped, which conserved heat on temporary stops. Two silencers of the Burgess straight-through type were now employed, which reduced noise without the creation of back-pressure. The fitting of a downdraught Stromberg carburettor with a semi-automatic choke control relieved the driver of the need to set the mixture by hand. The press were universally impressed by these changes. *The Autocar* of June 8th 1934, reviewing Humber Snipe 80 Sports Saloon remarked that:

"..(it) exercises an immediate charm over the motoring senses of the comparative stranger after the first hundred yards...

"This is a very remarkable car for its price."

The Pullman, with an 11ft chassis, was the largest in the range and had special springing which maintained riding comfort irrespective of the load carried. The setting of the rear shock absorbers could be adjusted by the driver by altering a control on the dash. To protect the car against theft, a steering lock was mounted in the column combined with the ignition switch. Operating in a way now familiar to modern drivers, the steering was locked once the ignition had been switched off and had

AN INTERESTING EXPERIMENT

1. In order to demonstrate the absence of pitching on an **Evenkeel** car, a beaker filled to within one inch of the rim with ink was placed on a sheet of blotting paper on the floor of the rear compartment. The **Evenkeel** car was then driven over colonial section at 20 m.p.h., and, as the photograph shows, only a minute quantity of ink was spilled.

2. The same test was carried out on a car fitted with **ordinary suspension** under exactly similar conditions at the same speed over the same track, but with the beaker only 2/3rds full of ink ; as the photograph shows, a considerable amount of ink was spilled.

Extract from the Rootes brochure explaining the Evenkeel suspension system. It is fortunate that The Trades Descriptions Act was not passed until 1968!

to be unlocked with a Yale key before it was possible to start the engine. The Lucas "Startix" automatic re-starting mechanism was also available as an option, which would restart the engine if it stalled.

The four-cylinder Twelve was improved in 1934 with the fitting of the Lucas "startix" electrical re-starting system as described above. New bodystyles included a "Vogue" saloon, a handsome two-door model displayed at Humber's stand at Olympia. A certain Captain Molyneaux, a notable British clothes designer of the period who worked in Paris, was employed by Humber as a styling consultant on this model, hence the name "Vogue". To complete the Twelve range, a smart two-door tourer was offered. In common with all Humber models for that season, a radio aerial was fitted in the roof as a standard item. From late 1934, the Twelve was fitted with an all-synchromesh gearbox (also used on the Hillman Minx) and a freewheel.

Prices varied from £265 for a Humber Twelve Saloon, to £895 for a Thrupp & Maberly-bodied Sedanca de Ville. These cars all sold well into 1935 when a new range was introduced with the "Evenkeel" independent suspension chassis-frame. "Evenkeel" was marketed separately as "The New Wonder Suspension", and was supposed to eliminate pitch and bumping, enhancing the comfort of rear passengers and eliminating rattles and noise. This was in fact independent front suspension by another name and the new transverse leaf arrangements were similar to those on the 1935 range of Studebakers. "Cushioned Power" was another phrase designed to glamorise the fact that the Humber engine and gearbox were now mounted on rubber blocks. The 1936 range also featured the "Vari-Load" rear suspension - which was little more than an extra leaf in the rear springs to absorb the weight of five passengers and their luggage, which worked!

De Normanville transmission, offered from Spring 1935 at £30 extra, was less of a success, despite the efforts of the Rootes publicity department, which dispatched the unfortunate Dudley Noble and an "automatic" Snipe fitted with the gearbox on a 5,000 mile trip to the Sahara, hauling a heavily equipped caravan. The de Normanville gear system was a form of semi-automatic gearchange operated from a gear lever on the steering wheel which projected towards the driver's right hand. On a quadrant, the various options were marked from bottom to top "R-N-1-2-3-4-C" "R" for reverse, "N" for neutral and "C" for "Coast". To operate the system, the clutch was depressed and the lever moved to the selected gear. Gear changes could then be made simply by pressing the clutch and moving the lever to the next required position. "Coast" was freewheel, which could be disengaged by moving the gear lever back to "4". Captain E de Normanville provided a "simple" explanation in non-technical language of its principles over 13 pages of an illustrated brochure on the system. The de Normanville was an elaborate epicyclic system, and there is no doubt in the writer's mind that de Normanville's tortured prose contributed to the relative scarcity of vehicles equipped with the option.

Further elaborate names were to appear in 1936, when a new engine, christened the "Dynamax", was revealed. The "Dynamax" was a newly developed side-valve 27 HP 4086cc engine, which delivered 100 b.h.p. at 3,400 r.p.m.

"Humber owners will experience a new "velvet" smoothness, greater silence and improved acceleration and entirely new standards of performance in accord with modern road requirements.." promised the publicity. All the Humber range were fitted with variations on the Dynamax design, which was also to be fitted to other vehicles in the Rootes group, including Commer lorries, until 1953. The engine had little in common with previous Humber side-valve engines. The cylinder head was now aluminium and delivered a high

The split windscreen, introduced for the 1936 season. The cars are Humber Pullmans.

Six-light Humber Snipe saloon, as seen at the 1935 Motor Show. This picture was probably taken as the Humber stand was being prepared.

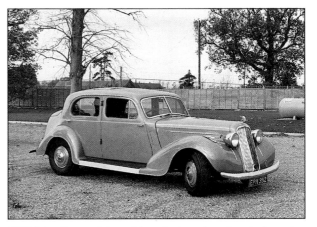

1936 Snipe Sports Saloon. Note the large boot bustle, featuring a built-in spare wheel. The boot lid was on top.

Cathedral Garage, Bristol. This publiciity shot was taken in 1937 for Humber Service Week, and features a Twelve saloon on the left and the larger Pullman on the right.

41

January 1938 edition of the *Rootes' Gazette*. The Rootes' organisation placed great emphasis on their international distribution network and produced an "in-house" magazine for circulation among the dealers. This was in several languages and carried articles on new Rootes products, publicity materials and selling techniques. This particular issue was promoting the Humber marque.

compression ratio of 6:1. The block was now one casting which accommodated the cylinders and the crankcase. With a four-main-bearing crankshaft, fully counterbalanced, performance was only matched by the very few expensive American imports.

In 1935, the big Humbers were completely redesigned. The *Evenkeel* suspension system was the work of designer Arther Booth, who had used a similar system for his previous employers, Studebaker. The Snipe, in particular, was aimed at the overseas markets, and it was important to demonstrate that the Humber was a comfortable and reliable vehicle in different road conditions. Accordingly, Dudley Noble, a journalist who

wrote extensively for Rootes' in-house magazine, *Modern Motoring*, was again despatched on several promotional continental tours, including eight days in a Swiss skiing resort (regarded as a somewhat exotic location by the British car-buyer of the 1930s), and visits to little-known parts of Yugoslavia, Bulgaria and Turkey.

The 16/60 model was dropped in favour of the new "Eighteen" with a new side-valve engine of 69.5mm x 120mm bore and stroke. A first for Humber was the provision of servo-assisted brake operation throughout the model range.

By the mid-1930s, certain transatlantic influences were becoming apparent in the external appearance of

Humber cars. This influence was of hardly surprising, since both Rootes brothers were frequent travellers to the United States in the 1920s and 1930s and as the world's most rapidly expanding industrial nation, the United States was the home of modern and progressive trends in motor vehicle technology and design.

It is no coincidence that the large Humbers from 1935 and 1936 onwards resembled the American Hudsons, Chryslers and Dodges, which also had large, six-cylinder engines. By 1936, this influence was clearly seen as Humbers adopted more "streamlined" styles with faired-in sidelights and vee-windscreens. To retain their British identity, however, the formal separate radiator grille, with chromium-plated bars topped by the "Snipe" mascot, was retained.

Humber cars were also favoured with Royal Patronage. The Duke of York (later King George VI) had taken delivery of two Humber Pullman Limousines in January 1933. Edward VIII favoured Humbers, and in August 1936 ordered a Humber Pullman Limousine for his personal and official use and granted the company a Royal warrant. This Pullman was a standard model with no special fittings and was finished in black with red coachlines. Powered by the 27 HP six-cylinder engine, it featured the much publicised Evenkeel suspension, which no less than Alec Issigonis helped to develop.

That particular vehicle, as well as several other Humber cars from the Royal Mews, saw service at the few official engagements that Edward VIII attended, including the opening of the Canadian War Memorial at Vimy Ridge, France on July 26th 1936. Following his abdication, the Duke of Windsor remained a Humber customer and had a number delivered to him while in exile in France. George VI also used Humbers on several state occasions after becoming King and the cars were frequently used to supplement the Royal Daimlers, providing transport for the Royal entourage.

This Royal patronage helped to establish Humber as the top people's car by the end of the 1930s. Humber also made efforts to publicise the sale of any of their vehicles to 1930s film stars such as Douglas Fairbanks Snr and Anna Neagle, making the large Humbers synonymous with the lifestyles of the rich and famous. Left hand drive Pullmans were also becoming established overseas as ambassadorial transport.

1937 saw some reorganisation of the Humber range, with the result that an entirely new 21 HP Snipe was announced, together with a new Sixteen, the Snipe Imperial and the Pullman. The Snipe and the Sixteen were virtually identical in external appearance, but there were a number of differences in specification, particularly the engines. The Sixteen had a 2576.5cc six-cylinder engine of 16.95 HP. The Snipe had a slightly larger 3180.9cc six-cylinder engine with a higher power rating of 20.9 HP. The main similarities were that both engines were side-valve designs, following 1930s Humber practice, and had aluminium alloy heads, four main bearings and a relatively high compression ratio.

One new development was the positioning of the engine mountings on a cross member supporting the gearbox, thus avoiding gear lever flutter, allowing for movement of the flexibly mounted engine. Clutch and accelerator were operated through flexible armoured cables, so that no movement of the major components would be transmitted to the driver's foot.

The recently established Evenkeel suspension had been simplified and improved, allowing the same standard of ride as the previous year's models on a shorter wheelbase. On the chassis was mounted a genuine five-seater all-steel body with a recessed roof for increased headroom and shaped front seats for increased rear-passenger leg-room. A new facia was used, with instruments being grouped around two dials directly in front of the driver. With a better performance than the old Snipe and a price reduction of £100, the 1937 models offered remarkable value for money, with the Sixteen saloon priced at £330 and the Snipe saloon at £345.

The larger models, the Snipe Imperial and the Pullman were now fitted with Stromberg carburettors with automatic choke. The new radiator had a deeper "V" and was squared-off at the top. Internally, the cabin was roomier with larger seats and improved sound insulation. Both were powered by the well-established six-cylinder, 4086cc, 27 HP engine. A choice of bodies for the Snipe Imperial was provided for the owner driver, with a basic saloon body, a saloon with division, 4-light saloon (with or without division) Sports saloon and Drop-Head Coupe, with prices ranging from £495 for the saloon to £555 for the Drop-Head Coupe. The Pullman was offered as a Limousine, Landaulette, Special Limousine, Special Landaulette and Sedanca de Ville with prices from £735 to £1,095.

With a total weight of around two tons, the performance of the larger Humbers was comparable with similar-sized American cars, the Snipe having an 80 m.p.h. top speed and 0-50 m.p.h. acceleration of 16.6 seconds.

The Autocar of September 1937, reviewing the new models concluded that: *"All through, in fact, comfort and silence have been predominating aims, coupled with a real high performance, and in these fine all-British cars will be found a really high degree of craftsmanship, performance and appearance."*

The continual upgrading of the Humber range, Royal patronage, a clever public relations department and attention to the overseas markets paid dividends by the mid-1930s. On 30th November 1937, *The Motor* noted that the net profits of the Humber company for the year ended July 31st 1937 had increased by £21,288 to £263,174. This was a sizable profit compared to the early 1930s and the company paid a 15% dividend to its shareholders. Although 1938 and 1939 in particular saw a fall in profits, the company continued to make money for its shareholders through to 1940, when a profit of £247,159 was announced.

Humber dealers were encouraged to seek out a wider range of customers towards the end of the 1930s. Recognising that car ownership was becoming more widespread, C H Fison, Chief Sales Executive of the Rootes group, wrote to dealers in the January 1938 issue of the *Rootes' Gazette* and stressed that:

"The Humber is a car with a magnificent tradition behind it....but with the new Humber programme offering wider values than ever before the policy of conservatism in selling needs considerable attention, and we must all take the fresh view-point of the

Humber to get out of our minds once and for all that it is a car appealing only to a comparatively small class of purchaser.

"Humber must be sold more aggressively. The days when the mountain came to Mohammed are gone; the approach must come from the Distributor and Dealer, and be direct and insistent. To sell on specification, performance and price can be just as dignified as selling merely on name - and far more effective."

The basic body shape of the Snipes and Pullmans was to continue until the 1940s. This featured a swept tail and an integral boot. The regular saloons and the sports versions had projecting boots, which were later replaced with slightly less cumbersome razor-edge styling.

1938 saw the addition of a further car to the Humber range, the "Super" Snipe. This had a better performance than any pre-war Humber model and followed the then popular formula of mating a lightweight chassis with a powerful engine. In this case the 27 HP 4086cc six-cylinder, side-valve engine was mounted on the 114in chassis of the Sixteen/Snipe of the previous year. A number of bodystyles were offered, but the most popular was a four-light razor edged sports saloon, which replaced the somewhat unbalanced shape of the previous year's models, with a standard saloon or drop head coupe being offered as alternatives. With a top speed of 85 m.p.h., the Super Snipe was priced at £385 and some 1,500 were sold that season. A larger boot was offered for the 1940 season, but the coming of the war resulted in only a few being produced that year. The car was very well received on its launch. A number of mechanical refinements had been added such as hydraulically operated brakes and the whole package was remarkable value for money.

The Autocar commented:

"... in this new model something altogether exceptional has been put into a car costing less than £400. It is capable of holding its own anywhere."

The bore and stroke of the Dynamax engine remained unchanged, but most of the other features of the engines were revised through 1939. A re-designed cylinder block, new camshaft and new externally-fitted oil pump to accommodate the newly positioned distributor and the radically rearranged ancillaries. The previous arrangement of timing chain driving into a distributor tower, fuel pump, then dynamo and water pump, all via one shaft, was abandoned and replaced by a fan belt driving a dynamo via it's pulley. In addition, a fan was mounted on the front of the water pump at the top of the block. With the oil pump now mounted externally, pick-up and delivery oil-ways were cast into the crankcase. Mounted under the distributor was a replaceable oil filter replacing the permanent strainers. All of these features were to contribute to the longevity and reliability of the engines.

Despite the declaration of war in September, Humber confidently announced a new 1940 range in *The Motor* on December 6th 1939. A number of changes were made to the external appearance of the entire range at the front and rear ends. A large lift-up boot was fitted and a new snap-type petrol filler cap was added

located on the rear of the nearside wing. At the front the radiator grille, shell and the snipe mascot were all modified to *"present a thoroughly modern appearance."* Running boards were deleted on the Super Snipe and the Sports Saloon models, and in all cases the interiors were upgraded with extensive use of polished wood and leather, adding to the air of luxury. Only the Pullman had any noteworthy modifications to it's chassis where hydraulic brakes were finally added and a new cross-braced frame was produced, resulting in a weight saving of some 5 cwt on the completed car. This resulted in a quite respectable performance, with 85 m.p.h. maximum speed, and 0-50 m.p.h. through the gears in 11.6 seconds, as quick as the American Buick or Hudson.

Prices were again keenly competitive; £385 bought a Humber Sixteen six light saloon, a six-light Snipe cost £395 and a four-light Snipe £415. The more powerful Super Snipe was offered in several popular bodystyles, a six-light saloon at £515, four-light saloon at £530, sports saloon at £575 and the foursome coupe at £580. The most expensive of the range, the New Pullman Limousine, with coachwork from Thrupp & Maberly, could be purchased for £825.

Optimism about the level of sales in 1940 was misplaced. Once it was clear that Britain was once again entering into a lengthy conflict, the British motor industry was directed towards military needs, and the private motorist would have to wait until 1946 before new models were once again made available.

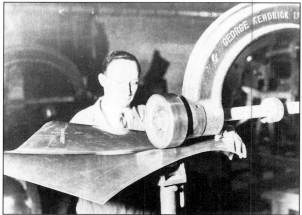

Coachbuilding at Thrupp & Maberly, Acton, circa 1939.

44

1939 Humber catalogue, with heavily retouched photos of the Sixteen, Super Snipe Sports Saloon and Sedanca de Ville.

5. HUMBER FIGHTING VEHICLES

Humber's development as a fighting vehicle manufacturer stemmed from the Rootes involvement in the shadow factory scheme. This scheme was a direct response to Air Staff misgivings about the build-up of military might in Hitler's Germany and the rise of fascist dictatorships, and, in September 1935, Air Marshall Sir Hugh Dowding advised Bristol's Roy Fedden that *"the air staff have come to the conclusion that we are going to have a war with Germany."* The Ministry plan was to put in place arrangements for the manufacture of vehicles and aircraft that would be required to deal with the military threat from overseas.

In Britain's motor industry of the 1930s the government saw the engineering expertise and the manufacturing capacity to deal with military needs effectively and it was concluded that the best way forward was to choose an established manufacturer with a product suited to the needs of the forces and replicate the production process elsewhere. Most of the motor manufacturers who were to be involved in the scheme had some experience of aircraft production from the First World War, including Humber, who had manufactured both aircraft and aero engines. From a military standpoint, this also meant that if production at one plant was disrupted by enemy action, other "shadow" plants could maintain supply.

The Bristol Mercury radial engine was the first unit chosen for this treatment and at a meeting held at the Bristol works, the Rootes brothers were among the representatives of the "big six" motor manufacturers invited to participate. It was proposed that the government would build and equip shadow factories and that the various manufacturers would be responsible for their running and their personnel. For this service they would be paid a £50,000 per annum management fee and £75 per engine. Roy Fedden of Bristol was later to recall that only William Rootes had any enthusiasm for this scheme, and this finally persuaded the other, more reluctant, manufacturers to take part.

Two Rootes shadow factories were built. The first at Aldermoor Lane, Stoke, behind its own factory, and the second at a 60-acre site in the village of Ryton-on-Dunsmore, 5 miles from Coventry. The best of Rootes management and engineering expertise were put into the shadow factories and by 1940, the group was producing 30% of all bomber aircraft. During the course of the war, the group was to produce some 11% of the UK output of wheeled vehicles which included 60% of armoured cars, 35% of all scout cars and 3,500 other reconnaissance vehicles as well as B.B.C. Recording Vans, Military Wagons and Ambulances.

One of the most notable cars to see service was a pre-war Humber Snipe that was used by a British Movietonews crew on the Italian Front between March 1943 and October 1944. With a strengthened roof and outsize wheels and tyres, this remarkable vehicle carried a ton of equipment, Paul Wyand and Michael Gray for over 30,000 miles, covering the bombing of Monte Casino, the link-up of the forces at Anzio and the filming of other, more famous Humbers used by Montgomery and Churchill.

The road cars used by the forces departed little from the specification for the civilian vehicles. The most widely seen car used by the army was the 27 HP Humber Snipe Staff Car. These were supplied in three basic body types, the most common being almost identical with the normal Super Snipe saloon, and the remaining choices being an open tourer and a partitioned limousine. The latter two had special bodies by Thrupp & Maberly, although the standard of finish was not what could be termed "Mayfair showroom order". With a comparatively unstressed engine and a high cruising speed, together with independent front suspension, these cars were chosen to equip the British forces because very few modifications to the standard specification were required. The most easily-seen modifications was the cutting away of the back of the body, fitting firmer springs to provide extra ground clearance when mounting ramps or traversing rough roads and the fitting of large section low pressure tyres. These unusual tyres provided a characteristic "whizzing" noise when the car moved at speed as well as remarkable adhesion.

The two most well-known Humber open tourer staff cars were allocated for use by General, (later Field Marshall) Sir Bernard Montgomery. The first was Humber car number M.239459, first used by Montgomery in October 1942, and subsequently used by him almost continuously during his service in North Africa. It later provided transport for the Prime Minister, Winston Churchill, in February 1943, when he visited the troops in Tripoli and His Majesty King George VI in June of the same year for use when reviewing the now victorious British troops. "Old Faithful" was later used in Sicily and Italy by Montgomery before being handed over to his successor, General Sir Oliver Leese. At the end of the

Rootes "Shadow" factory products. A 1937 Blenheim, Hillman 14 and Humber Snipe.

Montgomery in "Old Faithful" in Tripoli, North Africa.

war, the car was presented back to the company by the War Office as *"a token of the good service rendered by Humber vehicles to the war effort"*. The car was subsequently exhibited by Humber at the Rootes show-room in Piccadilly and in a number of locations around the country. The car has now been preserved for the nation and is exhibited at the Museum of Army Transport at Beverley, North Humberside.

A second Humber, M.439485, later known as "the Victory car", first made an appearance in Montgomery Street, Birmingham, and served Field Marshall Montgomery throughout his campaign on the Western Front in 1944. Writing to a member of the Rootes staff in August 1943, Montgomery said, with characteristic understatement that: *"I have travelled many hundreds of miles in my Humber car and will no doubt travel many more."* In fact, the Humber accompanied him for many tens of thousand miles on the campaigns through 1944 and 1945. This car, too, has been preserved and is now displayed at the Museum of British Road Transport, Coventry.

Humber staff cars were remarkably popular with the allied forces in Europe and Africa. An officer in East Africa recalled that *"I had an open Tourer 27 HP Humber Staff Car. It did 48,000 miles on very rough roads without one single breakdown and both my African driver and I became devoted to it."*

An *Autocar* war correspondent noticed that the American staff were particularly taken with the saloons and wrote:

"A fact that strikes me about the American sector of France is the number of British Staff Cars in use. The Americans are using Humber Pullman and Super Snipes extensively for this work and I learned that the general opinion of these cars is that they are very comfortable and suited to Continental roads. This expression of opinion from the Americans was all the more interesting, of course, in view of the fact that their standards are based on the use of their own big cars."

In addition to the staff cars, many of which varied

little from their pre-war civilian counterparts, Humber produced a whole range of other Military vehicles.

Heavy Utility was the description of the various large estate cars used mostly as staff cars by British and later Allied unit and formation commanders. The best-known and most common was the Humber "Box", so-named because of its square appearance. In its basic form, the Box contained a mapboard fitted to the rear of the front seats, a wide rear seat and two additional fold-down rear seats. Reading lamps, arm rests and a sliding roof were incorporated in cars for the use of staff officers. Many of these vehicles, which included the only British built 4 x 4 (four-wheel drive) Heavy Utilities as well as 4 x 2s, saw service until the late 1950s. A number were modified into open touring cars with fold-down canvas covers for use in North Africa and one of these conversions was immortalised in the opening sequence of the feature film "Ice Cold In Alex".

Other variations on the Heavy Utility were the *Light Ambulance*, 1,144 being produced and bodied by Thrupp & Maberly, which enabled 2 stretcher and 3 seating cases to be carried; a personnel carrier, with

1942 Four-Wheel-Drive Heavy Utility.

Humber Snipe Utility Car.

seating for three men and lockers for their equipment; the *F.F.W.* (Fitted For Wireless) and a specially-converted *B.B.C. Recording Van*.

The Recording Van was an extensively modified Light Ambulance used by B.B.C. war correspondents for the writing and recording of battlefront despatches. Capable of carrying living and sleeping equipment for a crew of three, personal baggage was carried on the body roof. These vehicles were profoundly uncomfortable but immensely tough. One B.B.C. correspondent in Italy reported that:

"Road conditions out here are terrible. At times the vehicle is on its side at an angle of 45 degrees. Perhaps for miles...Road shock is so bad that I have had to replace interior light bulbs weekly." Following the end of the war, these vehicles continued to be used by the B.B.C. for outside broadcasts, being well-suited for carrying heavy recording equipment.

Humber's first major contribution to the range of military fighting vehicles was to come after the Dunkirk evacuation. Both Humber and Standard were asked to produce a light armoured car.

A prototype, christened the "Humberette" was based on the Humber Super Snipe chassis and built during June 1940. After some slight modifications, including War Department pattern rims for "Runflat" tyres, the new armoured car was put into production in July 1940. Some two hundred were built and subsequently known as "Ironside 1".

Powered by the Humber 27 HP engine and weighing some 2 ¾ tons, these light open-topped armoured cars had a top speed of 45 m.p.h. The Ironsides were supplied in lieu of tanks and subsequently to equip armoured car regiments and the Reconnaissance Corps.

Ironsides were also used as armoured transport for Cabinet ministers and members of the Royal Family. Initially designed to provide a safe means of escape in the event of the expected German invasion in 1940. The invasion was expected to be initiated by air attacks followed by widespread parachute troop landings, and these fast, light reconnaissance cars were an ideal choice for an escape vehicle.

Following trials with the old Lanchester 40 HP armoured car, Humber Special Ironside armoured saloons were supplied to the 12th Royal Lancers. Although reasonably comfortable, these vehicles had no windows at first and after the first batch was delivered in September 1940, small bullet proof windows were to be provided. The first car was delivered on 13th September 1940, a second five days later. Shortly after delivery, King George VI and Queen Elizabeth, as well as Winston Churchill, used these cars. By January 1941, the prospects of invasion had lessened and two Humber Protected Snipe Saloon Cars were delivered. Although conventional in appearance, these were armour-plated with austenitic steel panels against small arms fire and shell splinters. Being much more comfortable than the Special Ironsides, these cars eventually replaced the original Ironsides, although these older vehicles were used as escort vehicles until the end of 1941.

The Ironside Mark I was followed by a Mark II which had an enclosed roof mounting a small turret, which was in turn followed by the similar-looking Mark III. However, the Mark III introduced four-wheel drive, and was itself succeeded by the Mark IIIA, which had a number of minor modifications, the most immediately noticeable being the extra observation ports. This 3 ½ ton vehicle was powered by the 27 HP six-cylinder side-valve engine, giving a top speed of 50 m.p.h. Armament consisted of a 0.303 Bren light machine gun mounted in the turret, with the occasional addition of a .55-in Boys anti-tank rifle mounted to the front of the hull. With a light armour of 10mm, these cars usually had a crew of three.

Humber armoured cars were the most numerous of British fighting vehicles to be produced in World War II, some 5,000 being produced between 1940 and 1945. Several variants were designed. The first Humber Armoured Car was virtually identical in appearance to the

Mark I Scout Car.

Mark II Armoured Car.

Guy Mark 1A Armoured Car, although the mechanical components were pure Humber. A number of suggestions were made by the services for improvements and these were introduced in the Mark II. Of a relatively minor nature, these midifications consisted of a neatened front end, a redesigned radiator intake and the incorporation of the driver's visor in the glacis plate.

More radical improvements to the Humber Armoured Car Mark III had been made by the time it was introduced in 1942. A more roomy turret allowed the crew to be increased from three to four. However, the two Besa machine-guns, which featured in all the Humber armoured cars to date, were later replaced by the American 37mm gun, which once again reduced the crew from four to three. All Humber Armoured Cars weighed some 7 tons and the ubiquitous 27 HP six-cylinder engines gave a top speed of 45 m.p.h. Primarily used by the armoured regiments and reconnaissance regiments, they saw service in most theatres of war where British and Commonwealth troops were engaged, but particularly in North Africa and the Middle East.

Whilst production of the Daimler Scout Car was continued through out the war and beyond, the 6,665 produced were insufficient to meet the demands of the

Mark III Armoured Car.

forces and Humber was asked to design a scout car which could be used to supplement the Daimler. Some 4,200 Humber Scout Cars were built between 1942 and the end of the war. To avoid unnecessary production complications and interchangeability of components as far as possible the Humber Scout Car Mark I employed many of the components used in existing Humber military vehicles, but with some adaption for the rear engine layout. The 27 HP six-cylinder engine

Mark II Light Reconnaissance Car.

8 cwt. 4 x 2 "Fitted For Wireless" on Snipe chassis.

was again utilised and linked to a four-speed gearbox which gave a top speed of 60 m.p.h. The Humber was slightly larger than the Daimler and mechanically less sophisticated, with less armour, which resulted in the armoured regiments preferring the Humbers for liaison purposes rather than scouting. A Mark II Scout Car was later developed, which was visually almost identical to the Mark I, but included synchromesh to the 2nd as well as 3rd and 4th gears.

Whilst in the early part of the war, Daimler and Humber vehicles were developed independently, with little co-ordination between the companies, it was decided in 1943 to develop a further armoured vehicle which was a compromise between the advanced Daimler and the orthodox Humber. Humber was entrusted with the overall coordination of design of the new vehicle, designing the hull, turret and stowage arrangements. Daimler dealt with the design of the suspension and steering, which was similar to the existing Daimler armoured cars, incorporating independent springing and forward and rearward steering. Commer, a Humber subsidiary, was charged with the design of the gearbox, transfer box and axles. The power unit was an American RX series engine from Hercules Motor Corp., a six-cylinder side-valve 9.1 litre unit, being primarily chosen because no British petrol engine of a comparable size was easily available. The Coventry was a larger, roomier vehicle than either the Daimler or the Humber, with a four man crew, commander, gunner, loader and driver. With a QF 2-pounder gun, 7.92mm Besa machine gun and twin Vickers .303 anti aircraft machine-guns, this was a formidable fighting vehicle.

Production of the Coventry I began in 1944, with an initial order of 1,150 being placed by the War Office. However, by this time there were ample stocks of both the Daimler and Humber armoured cars and very few were built. Some prototypes of a proposed Coventry II were made, being an up-gunned modification, but very few were made out the fifty ordered. A Coventry III never got beyond the planning stage with the decision of the

Tank Board that production should cease as soon as possible after the cessation of hostilities.

Other experimental Humber armoured vehicles included the Humber Gnat, with a high hull and a small turret, but no mudguards, which was to the same general specification of the Morris Salamander, the Humber Hexanaut, a 15cwt Airportable Floater and the Karmann-bodied Super Snipes, based on the Super Snipe chassis, with a beetle-backed body and Humber grille. The Hexanaut was a load carrier developed through 1942 and 1943, which was to be capable of being carried by air transport and dropped by parachute to the battle zones. Though not truly an amphibian, it was capable of work in calm water, but appeared to be more at home on jungle tracks. Comprising a narrow space-frame steel box, or hull, the vehicle was eleven feet long, with a forward sloping bow and six tightly mounted tractor-type wheels. Propelled by a pair of 14 HP Humber engines, the two engines drove a set of wheels on each side, but the vehicle was never fully developed and only three were made.

Following the end of hostilities, the Wilhelm Karmann coachbuilding concern of Onsabruck, West Germany was chosen to rebody damaged Snipe staff cars under Allied forces control. Completely new Karmann-designed "beetle back" style 4-door saloon bodies were fitted to the chassis. It is not known how many were built but one was owned by a *Post Vintage Humber Car Club* member in Finland in the mid-1970s.

A curious episode involved Humber and Volkswagen. Following the battle of El Alamein, a VW Type 82 reconnaissance vehicle was sent to Humber for technical analysis. The report entitled *"Report on Examination of German Light Aid Detachment Vehicle Type V.W. 82 Volkswagen"* took eight months to compile and, despite wartime austerity, was published on 64 pages of glossy foolscap paper, bound in cloth hard covers. The Humber technicians had weighed the VW, taken it apart piece-by-piece, analysed all the parts and drawn a number of conclusions about VW's production

Karmann-bodied Snipe.

Rear view of the Kharmann-bodied Snipe.

methods. It was noted that:

"*Extensive use is made of aluminium and magnesium base alloys, and a very good finish is imported to the die castings.*"

"*The design is particularly interesting because it is quite uninfluenced by any previous traditions, and it is doubtful if the question of whether the public would or would not like a car with an air-cooled engine positioned at the rear was considered by the designer.*"

"*Looking at the general picture, we do not consider that the design represents any special brilliance, apart from certain of the detail points, and it is suggested that it is not to be regarded as an example of first class modern design to be followed by the British Industry.*"

This was none other than the military version of the Volkswagen Beetle. By 1947, production of this car had reached 8,987 and by 1959, production was up to 575,407, and the Beetle eventually became the world's best selling car. In 1947, the Rootes Group was given the opportunity to buy the Volkswagen plant, but it seemed that they were not at all interested. Ironically, it was the disastrous attempt to produce a rear engined car in the 1960s which was to result in the group's eventual collapse. Had Rootes decided to purchase the VW plant when it was offered to him in 1947, it is quite possible that the Imp project would never have been undertaken.

With end of the Second World War, Humber fighting vehicle production was ended with the exception of the FV1600 series of combat range trucks. 15cwt trucks in various guises were based on the American Dodge 4 x 4 weapons carriers, with Austin producing a variant which went into production in Canada in 1944 and 1945, though it never reached volume production stage. With the end of hostilities this project was cancelled but a standardised high-mobility vehicle was still required by the military. The Ministry of Supply and the Rootes group commenced work on such a project in 1947 and by 1950 prototypes were being tested. Five main classes of trucks were created by the British authorities ranging from ¼ ton to 10-ton payload class vehicles, comprising three basic patterns; CT or Combat, tactical all-wheel drive high mobility vehicles; GS or General Service, all-wheel drive militarized commercial vehicles and CL, off-the-shelf commercial vehicles. CT were a purely military pattern which could be given to any truck manufacturer. Powered by standardized Rolls-Royce engines, there were several derivatives, but all designated FV1600.

Because of the expense of CT trucks, CT schemes were eventually terminated, but the Humber FV1600 series was particularly notable, with fully independent suspension, water-proofing, electrical suppression and fully tropicalised components. Much of the component manufacturing for these vehicles was sub-contracted to

1950s FV1600 Wireless Truck.

Humber one-ton Armoured Car, known as the "Pig". These are still used by British forces in Northern Ireland

Rootes subsidiaries and other manufacturers, though to Humber's specification. Whilst not exclusively a Humber product, the FV1600 was officially designated "Humber" but using the Roll-Royce six-cylinder petrol engine. Volume production of the FV1600 series continued through 1952 and 1953 and some 3,700 units were assembled at the former shadow factory at Ryton-on-Dunsmore and at GKN Sankey at Telford Shropshire, and delivered by 1954. Comparatively few trucks were issued to the services and most were placed into storage for future use.

From this large stock, many one-tonners were commandeered for conversion for special roles. The first was the Humber FV1602 F.F.W., the "F.F.W." being "Fitted For Wireless", with a special two-speed generator being fitted to charge the wireless batteries. A more advanced FV1604 F.F.W. was later produced for HF and VHF radio sets. A further early variant was an FV1609 armoured truck, primarily designed as a lightly armoured troop-carrier, being easily adapted for a number of roles in all the armed services. By 1960, further armoured conversions were commissioned including FV1611, an armoured personnel/cargo carrier; FV1612 F.F.W.; FV1613 ambulance, with accommodation for three stretchers or eight sitting patients or one stretcher and four sitting patients.

Approximately 1,700 of the original Humbers were converted to armoured vehicles, and some 500 seeing service in Northern Ireland. Generally known as the "Pig", re-armouring in the 1970s resulted in the AFVs weight increasing from 4,200kg to 6,000kg and the Ulster "Pigs" were and still are a common feature in the province. These in turn have been the subject of a number of conversions, the "Kremlin Pig", which has wire mesh side-skirts to protect against hand-held rocket launchers and other munitions, the "Flying Pig", which has large side screen for anti-riot work and the "Holy Pig" which has perspex screen around the hatch in the roof of the vehicle. In addition, a small number of Humber Trucks were converted for towing Green Archer mortar-locating equipment and as an anti-tank missile carrier, the FV1620 "Hornet".

A number of surplus vehicles were disposed of from 1963 to 1965 via Ruddington disposal auctions, with some being auctioned later during 1968 and 1969. Most of these were used as light breakdown recovery vehicles and for other special purposes, including one used by Chipperfields Circus for capturing wildlife for zoos. Another example in more recent years had a 1960s Super Snipe body fitted to the chassis! .

Some surplus FV1600s were sold off as recovery trucks and agricultural vehicles.

6. POST-WAR DEVELOPMENTS

By the end of the Second World War, 1% of Britain's working population was employed by the Rootes group. For his efforts in the shadow factory scheme, William Rootes was knighted and Reginald some time later. Several other members of the family were appointed to key positions in the group, including Geoffrey and Brian Rootes, William's sons and Timothy, Reginald's son. The end of hostilities allowed Rootes to return to the manufacture of civilian motor cars and for this purpose the two shadow factories were taken over from the government. The plants were converted from military to civilian motor vehicle manufacture. With increasing emphasis on overseas markets, plans were put in hand to export to 79 countries at a cost of £7½ million. A number of steps were taken which included the establishment of a motor factory in Australia building C.K.D.s (completely-knocked-down, that is, kits packed and sent from the UK) and the formation of concessionaire companies in cities such as New York and Rio de Janerio.

This expansion overseas was a sound move and by 1948 Rootes exports were worth in the region of £15 million per annum, twice the 1946 level. This steady flow of income allowed Rootes companies such as Humber to develop their Post-War programme of new cars in a relatively short time and a whole range of all-new models appeared in the late 1940s. This was extremely important, since the conditions in the home market in this period were far from ideal. In 1938, Britain had exported only 18-20% of motor car output, mostly to the commonwealth countries. In 1946 over 86,000 of 219,162 new cars went abroad, but by 1947 over 50% were exported, rising to 65% by 1950. The government exhortations to "export or die" suited the Rootes group, since they had always placed a heavy emphasis on overseas markets, long before the govern-

Winston Churchill at a Post-War rally in a 1946 Super Snipe Cabriolet.

Mark I Super Snipe Estate built for Queen Mary by Thrupp & Maberly. This featured an attendants's seat in the rear and was originally supplied as a "van" in order to qualify for extra petrol coupons! The wooden panels shown in the interior shot could be unclipped and removed to convert the "van" into an Estate Car. The vehicle was used at Sandringham and was sold and re-registered by Stratstones in 1951.

Mark I Hawk. The Mark II was identical in appearance but featured a column gearchange.

1947 Mark I Pullman Landaulette.

1946 Super Snipe Police Car used by the Metropolitan Police. Super Snipe Police cars also featured heavily in the Ealing film production "The Blue Lamp".

Snipe chassis with an all-steel safari or pick-up body for use on oil pipelines, mines, plantations etc. The commercial coachwork was by Reall of Ealing.

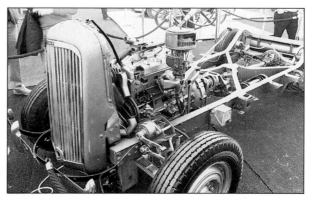

1946 Super Snipe chassis. This was used by the Wiltshire Police Traffic Division as a training aid. An electric motor simulated the workings of the engine, gearbox and final drive.

1946 Pullman Sedanca de Ville. The coachwork was by H J Mulliner included a number of interesting features to the interior appointments. Concealed diffused lighting was fitted behind the rear seat, the division was electrically controlled and the rear compartment featured a wireless, heater, occasional seats and a heater.

The 1948 Mark II Humber Pullman. "Exceptional comfort is provided for six passengers and driver, and, if necessary, an additional passenger may be carried in the both front and rear compartments. Provision is made for fitting "His Master's Voice Automobile Radio", also heating and air conditioning at extra charge."

Publicity photo of the Mark II Super Snipe.

1948 saw the phasing out of the pre-war designs. This period advert is probably one of the last to feature the Mark I Super Snipe and Snipe.

1949 Mark II Pullman Newspaper Delivery Van. These featured rubber wings and wood-framed steel-panelled bodywork.

1949 Pullman Mark II as used by the B.B.C. These cars had specially reinforced rear springs to withstand the weight of the recording equipment used by the Outside Broadcast Units.

ment. In the meantime, the British market had endured petrol rationing, in force until 1950; and a purchase tax of 33.3% for new vehicles under £1,000 and 66.6% for vehicles costing more than £1,000 in 1947. This artificially inflated prices of new cars beyond the reach of many. Fortunately, the Horsepower Tax disappeared in 1946, thus allowing some innovation in engine design and power output.

In common with other British manufacturers in the immediate Post-War period, the "new" Humber range of cars for 1946 differed little from those announced by Rootes for the 1940 season. These were announced in August 1945, before the end of hostilities in Japan, and the speed with which this was done was quite remarkable, although some development work may have been done before being officially allowed by the government. Production, though not radical development, was only just possible, because quota systems were still in operation, and sheet steel was still strictly rationed. The Super Snipe and the Pullman were joined, however, by one

Tickford-bodied Super Snipe Mark II Drophead Coupe.

new model with a four-cylinder 1944cc 14 HP engine, the Humber Hawk, a replacement of the Hillman 14 HP of 1940. The Hawk was built on a 9ft 6in chassis frame, with Evenkeel independent front suspension. A major policy change was introduced with the Hawk. Whereas pre-War, customers had been able to chose between several different bodystyles, on the Humber Hawk only the Pressed Steel company bodyshell was available. The Hawk Mark II was a development of the Mark I introduced in 1947, featuring the same bodystyle, but incorporating a column gearchange.

One other "Humber" product was a Mark I Hillman Minx in everything but name. A 1946 "Humber Ten" was assembled by Todd Motors in Wellington, New Zealand, where similar cars had been made since 1936. Only the Humber motif on the Humber-style radiator grille distinguished it from the small Hillman. This

practice was to continue on all Hillmans imported up to the 1960s.

The Snipe was similar to the 1940 model, but was now fitted with the 2731cc engine previously fitted in the Humber 18 HP of 1937. Technically it was similar in other respects to the Hawk, and was also only available with the Pressed Steel bodyshell. The Super Snipe and the Pullman, though broadly similar to their 1940 predecessors, had had some attention paid to noise insulation, the exclusion of draughts and greater passenger comfort, possibly with the American market in mind. A further 2in was added to the Pullman limousine to provide additional leg-room for the rear passengers and some minor detailed changes were made to it's rear end.

The Motor, commenting on these developments on August 15th, 1945 noted that:

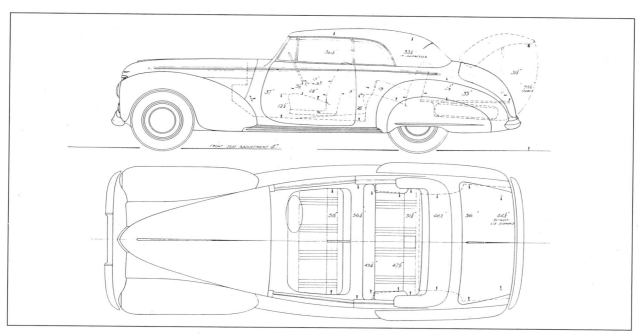

Tickford-bodied Super Snipe Mark II (the "Mark 2 ½") Drophead Coupe. These later cars had side lights rather than the auxilliary lamps.

"In short, these Humbers deserve the consideration of all those whose predilections run to something a little larger than the typical British light car. The various models provide too, a range of performance from good to excellent, with running costs to match."

In 1947, H J Mulliner built a few Pullman Sedanca de villes with full-flow wings and electric divisions, but at £2,300, this was not a best-seller and Thrupp & Maberly were commissioned to produce a design for the replacement Pullman Mark II for 1948. The coachbuilding firm had now abandoned the traditional side of its coachbuilding business and no further specially commissioned bodies were built for other manufacturers. However, Thrupp & Maberly concentrated on the Humber Pullmans and were used by other members of the Rootes group to produce convertibles and estate cars.

1948 saw the first post-War Motor Show and a number of new models were timed for release at that show. The Humber Hawk Mark III, as revealed in October 1948, featured a full-width bodystyle, faired-in headlamps and a four-light saloon instead of three-light. Interior space was increased although the wheelbase was somewhat shorter than its predecessor and the

1951 Mark III Pullman with coachwork by Castle Bodies Limited. Called the "Warwick", only one survives.

Evenkeel suspension system had been replaced by conventional coil springs and wishbones. The chassis frame of the Hawk was composed of box section side members, contrasting with the Snipe, which continued with cruciform cross bracing. With a completely new chassis and full width styling, the new Hawk Mark III was announced at the Earls Court Motor show and remained unchanged only until September 8th 1950, when the company announced the release of a new, more powerful, Hawk Mark IV. This previously heavy, underpowered car was fitted with an enlarged side-valve engine, which at 2267cc had better acceleration and increased torque at low speeds, a considerable improvement on the previous model's 1944cc engine. The Mark IV could be easily identified by the new separate sidelights at the front. The maximum speed was just over 70 m.p.h., which to some extent, met criticism about the previous model's performance, and fuel consumption was improved to 25 m.p.g. Overdrive was also offered as a catalogued option until the Hawk was phased out in 1957.

The Super Snipe and the Pullman were updated. The Pullman Mark II was extended from 127in to a 131in wheelbase, prompting the remark from *The Motor* that: *"..the car is designed to be handled by a professional chauffeur."*

59

Super Snipe Mark IV prototype. The then Managing Director, Bill Hancock, took it to Italy in 1949. Note that the body is essentially Mark IV Hawk with "Hawk" badges on the doors, but featuring the extended nose section to incorporate the newly-developed overhead-valve "Blue Riband" six-cylinder engine.

THE HUMBER HAWK

THE HUMBER HAWK

1950 Hawk Mark IV. Apart from the sidelights there was little to distinguish this car from the Mark III.

1951 Mark III Pullman Shooting Brake by Tickford.

With the Humber Snipe having been discontinued in summer 1948, the Humber Super Snipe was revised for the 1949 season and became the Humber Super Snipe Mark II. Mechanically, few changes were made, save that the wheelbase was lengthened by 3.5in and the track widened. New gearbox casings and linkages were added and the column gearchange was now standard. Major changes were made to the bodywork. A major front-end facelift was applied to the Pressed-Steel bodyshell by the Loewy studio, who now brought the appearance of the Super Snipe in line with the Thrupp & Maberly Pullman limousine. Although the passenger cabin was unchanged, a long narrow bonnet, with a new nose incorporated revised wings with the headlamps faired-in. Running boards made their first appearance since 1940 and alternative bodies, such as a touring limousine and luxury drop-head coupe by Tickford, were now available.

The Tickford Humbers were built in limited numbers between August 1949 and July 1950. Probably no more than 100 were built, at a cost to the customer of £1,993, including purchase tax. These coupes were

fitted with a three-position hood, a choice of four exclusive colours, figured Walnut facia and the finest Connolly hide interior.

The size and structural strength of the Humber Pullman did not go unnoticed by the B.B.C., who purchased some specially modified Pullmans with a reinforced suspension. Before the widespread use of magnetic tape, sound broadcasts were recorded on large 78 r.p.m. discs.

This presented a number of practical problems with outside broadcasts as the equipment was particularly heavy and cumbersome. Two 6-volt battery units were carried in the boot, one on either side of two enormous cable drums carrying 100 yards of cable and a microphone stand. In the rear passenger compartment, the recording turntable was installed, together with the amplifier and a talkback microphone. Despite the size and weight of the equipment, these units attended most of the outside broadcasts until 1955. These cars supplemented the F.F.W. Recording Vans, which had been in use since the war.

In 1950 Maurice Gatsonides took a standard 1950

1952 Super Snipe Mark III. This car was used by Bristol's Fire Chief.

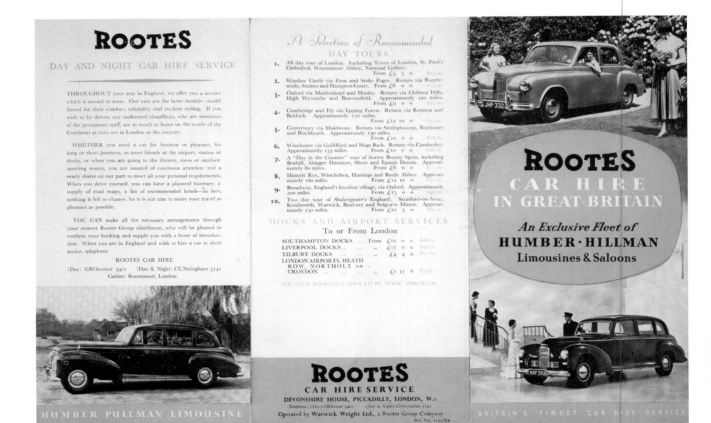

Rootes Car Hire.

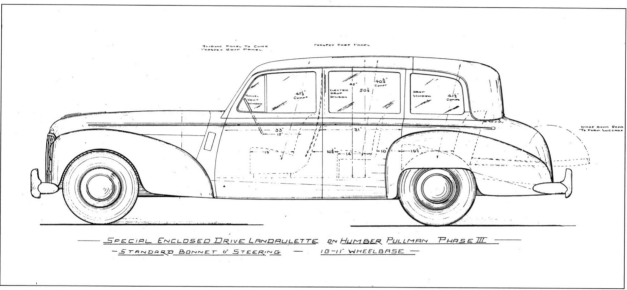

SPECIAL ENCLOSED DRIVE LANDAULETTE on HUMBER PULLMAN PHASE III

STANDARD BONNET & STEERING — 18-11" WHEELBASE —

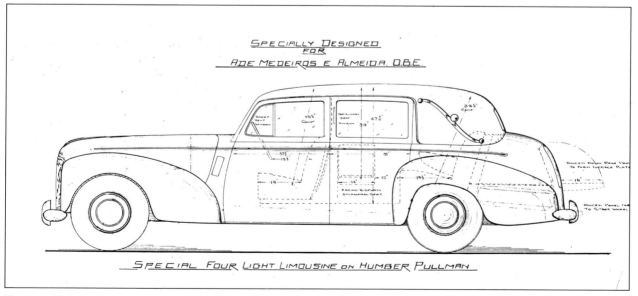

SPECIALLY DESIGNED
FOR
A DE MEDEIROS E ALMEIDA. O.B.E.

SPECIAL FOUR LIGHT LIMOUSINE on HUMBER PULLMAN

Thrupp & Maberly coachwork on a Pullman Mark III chassis. The lead car is a Special Enclosed Drive Landaulette. The second drawing is of another special design by Thrupp & Maberly, a four-light Limousine with an electric division and inward-facing occasional seats, a very unusual feature.

Royal Tour Cars. This photo shows the first of the Pullman Landualettes and Cabriolet for the 1948 tour of Australia and New Zealand on test. Because of the King's ill-health, the Tour was cancelled.

1951 Festival of Britain. Princess Elizabeth visited Norwich. A procession of five Pullmans and a 1948 Landaulette, driven by Mr John Mitchell, a senior Humber chauffeur, passed by Norwich Motor Co. Ltd, the local Rootes agent.

The Royal Tour of Australia and New Zealand in 1952 featured these Humber Pullman Cabriolets, originally built in 1948.

The 1948 Pullman Mark II Cabriolets again featured in the Royal Tour of Australia in 1954. Here the Queen and the Duke of Edinburgh are seen at Toomoomlea, Queensland on 11th March. The photo was commissioned by Gordon Motors, the local Rootes dealer.

1952 Hawk publicity material

Mark II Super Snipe on the Monte Carlo Rally. The 1950 Rally was one of the coldest ever, and the Humber departed from the Monte Carlo Casino on 20th January in dry weather and arrived in Luxemburg where they met the official Rootes team. In his book *Rallies and Races,* William Leonard recalls that there was:

"a lot of friendly teasing amongst the Rootes team members who respectfully, but not without a little scepticism, lifted their caps to the big brother Humber, which they expected to arrive in Monte Carlo a few weeks later. 'A very nice car' said somebody appreciatingly 'I shall certainly buy one when I am about eighty.' Within a week he was making inquiries about the price...."

The Humber performed remarkably well throughout the rally and at one point was set to take first place. However, the weight of the car, which had contributed to its steady roadholding throughout in treacherous conditions, eventually mitigated against it, and it was beaten into second place at the Mont des Mules. Nevertheless, a respectable performance for such a large and heavy car.

The Super Snipe was again revised in August 1950 as the Mark III. The bodystyle and the chassis were basically unchanged, except for the new revised bumpers and overriders for the first time. In addition, a Panhard locating rod was added to the rear suspension

and detachable rear wheel covers were added to the rear. Reviewing the Super Snipe in March 1951, the *Autocar* said:

"A distinctive place in the scheme of British cars as a whole is occupied by the Humber Super Snipe, as it is one of the very few big-bodied cars, with a quite large six-cylinder engine, available at well under £1,000 list price on the home market...."

"There is much to be said in favour of this model, with its ambitious specification, carried out in good style. It is a by no means unwieldy five-six seater of impressive appearance and clean modernized lines without saying anything extreme about them..."

The Super Snipe proved to be popular with the Police, though oddly enough, the most publicised use of a Humber Super Snipe by the Police at this time was an entry in the 1951 Monte Carlo Rally. Driven by R P Minchin, the Deputy Commander of the Metropolitan Police, with co-drivers Skeggs and Teer of the Police Driving School, the car handled well on the road section to Monte Carlo but was not quick enough in the acceleration and braking tests to qualify for the final run around the Grand Prix circuit. Two other Humber Super Snipes were entered, the both starting from Glasgow, driven by a team from Northern Ireland. The other Humber competitor was a Humber Hawk driven by H Pilmore-Bedford and R M Carter.

The Humber Pullman Limousine

Typical of the finest English carriagework, the Humber Pullman Limousine combines the qualities of a dignified town carriage with a capacity for fast, comfortable, long distance touring. It is a car of character and enduring quality, an example of that craftsmanship which is to-day all the more noticeable by its rarity.

True to a tradition founded in 1760, the coachwork by Thrupp and Maberly, one of the oldest and most skilled Coachbuilders, provides a unique combination of comfort, beauty and distinction. Humber engineering ensures the high quality of the Chassis and Power Unit.

The smoothness and steadiness of the ride over all types of road surface, and the absence of any tendency to sway when corners are taken at speed, is one of the most pleasant features of this car, and one for which the Humber Pullman has long been famous. This is due in large measure to the proved system of Evenkeel Independent Front Wheel Suspension pioneered by Humber, and to the provision of the torsion-bar sway eliminator and transverse stabiliser at the rear of the chassis.

This model incorporates many important advances in design, and is fitted with every accessory and feature necessary to ensure luxurious travel.

Humber Pullman Limousine catalogue from 1952. In common with other manufacturers of the time, Humber used considerable artistic license with representations of the lines of their vehicles.

Super Snipe Mark IV, 1952. Rootes originally acquired Humber to appeal to the middle and upper income brackets. This policy continued even in the immediate post-War period of austerity.

The large Humber Super Snipes and Pullmans of 1951, with their long wheelbase provided the basis for a number of fine coachbuilt bodies. The Super Snipe Mark III was then available in touring limousine form, with a division between front and rear compartments.

Castle Bodies (Coventry) Limited of Kenilworth, Warwickshire, produced a six-light estate car based on the Pullman chassis with the body framework in ash or oak, internally panelled in the same materials. With the rear seat up, 16 square feet of floor space was available, which grew to an enormous 38 square feet once the rear seats were folded down. Priced at £1,460 plus £834 purchase tax, delivery was within ten to twelve weeks of receipt of the chassis.

With a top speed of around 80 m.p.h. the Pullman Mark II sold surprisingly well, some 800 per year, and the later Pullmans were fitted with syncromesh bottom gears. The Pullman was also fitted with a division and

the front seats were trimmed in leather while the rear compartment was trimmed in the more exclusive West of England cloth.

The Humber Imperial was of the same mechanical specification as the Humber Pullman, but designed for the owner driver needing a large, 9-seater saloon. These were easily distinguished by the absence of a glass partition and the addition of leather trim in the front and rear compartments.

Some minor detailed mechanical changes were made to the Pullman and Imperial with the introduction of the Mark III in January 1951.

The limousine was remarkably easy to handle and one reviewer commented that "*it is a shock to glance over one's shoulder and be reminded afresh of the sheer size of the rear compartment*". Reviewing the Humber Pullman Limousine in June 1952, *The Motor* had taken the opportunity to put it through its paces at the 1952 M.C.C. Edinburgh Rally from Harrogate to Carlisle, competing with smaller, more orthodox saloons. The Humber proved to be more than equal to the task and was able to keep up with the field, particularly through the Honister Pass in the Lake District, where the steep climb was easily completed in second and third gears. This manner of driving was one which few, if any limousines were subjected to, yet *The Motor* was able to report that:

"*.. the Pullman has a most satisfying reserve of power and ...its handling qualities are outstandingly good. On corners it follows the precise line chosen with no undue effort on the wheel...a nicely balanced compromise between harsh ride and undue softness..*"

At a basic price of £1,600, this highly refined 9-seater vehicle was:

"*..unusual value for money just as, from the point of view of both passengers and driver, it represents an*

1952 Mark III Super Snipe.

London to Cape Town. Pictured at Hyde Park Corner on 26th November 1952 are Robbie Walshaw, George Hincliffe and Rootes representatives.

Walshaw and Hincliffe at E H Pickford, the Rootes dealer, after the trial.

Less glamourous, but necessary testing, a Mark II Super Snipe oil company development vehicle is put through its paces.

Mark IV Snipe pick-up.

This Mark IV Super Snipe pick-up was owned by the Kuwait Oil Company and is still in use today.

Humber continued to sponsor entrants for the Monte Carlo rallies. This 1954 Super Snipe was driven by George Murray-Frame and John Pearman.

Oslo to Lisbon in 90 hrs

Humber Super Snipe establishes new record—
beats time and weather in midwinter dash

This was a sensational trial of speed and endurance. A Humber Super Snipe—straight off the production line—raced from Oslo to Lisbon, through 15 countries, in 90 hours, including time for frontier stops. 3,280 miles, through winter blizzards, over ice-covered roads and mountain passes, the last 1,200 miles at an average speed of 50 miles per hour!

* * *

The Humber Super Snipe in this trial was driven by racing drivers Stirling Moss and Leslie Johnson, with John Cutts as navigator. They set off from Oslo at 02.00 hours on December 2, 1952. Their route lay from Norway through Sweden, Denmark, Germany, Holland, Belgium, Luxembourg, France, Switzerland, Leichtenstein, Austria, Italy, Jugoslavia, Monaco and Spain to Lisbon, in Portugal. The target set was 5 days at an average speed of 40 m.p.h. They finished by knocking 30 hours off this time and added 10 m.p.h. to the average speed. In face of all the difficulties and abnormal weather.

* * *

It was freezing hard when the Humber Super Snipe left Oslo at 02.00 hours on December 2. By 08.23 hours the same day they were in Gothenburg, Sweden. By 07.00 hours the next day they were in Germany and arrived in Dusseldorf at 09.40 hours on December 3.
The drivers had completed the first 1,000 miles on schedule, although the weather had gone from bad to worse. In Sweden, Denmark and Germany they battled with icy and fog-bound roads—even blizzards. The Humber Super Snipe behaved magnificently all the time, tirelessly kept up the set average of 40 m.p.h.
By 11.20 hours on December 3, the car arrived in Holland. Here, and through Belgium, visibility was better but roads were still ice-bound. Luxembourg was reached on schedule at 11.55 hours and the north-west corner of France swiftly traversed. The Swiss frontier was crossed at 20.45 hours and the car arrived in Zurich, the half-way point, at the scheduled time of 22.40 hours. 1,656 miles had been eaten up without the slightest trouble or fault developing in the Humber Super Snipe.

At 19.35 hours on December 4, the Humber Super Snipe arrived in Brescia, Italy, after a triumphant battle against appalling weather in the snow-covered mountain passes. Stopping only for the essential frontier formalities, the drivers, with endurance equal to the car, pressed on to Trieste. From Trieste into Yugoslavia, then back to Italy, through Milan and Genoa into Southern France.

* * *

At 08.30 hours on December 5, the car reached Monte Carlo. This was the last day of the epic drive. Despite the formidable strain of the trial, the Humber Super Snipe was still on schedule and on the top of its form.
From Monte Carlo the route was still arduous, winding through the dust of Southern France and the serpentine valleys of the Pyrenees. But the Spanish frontier was reached, Spain crossed and the car entered into Portugal. It arrived at Villar Formoso, the objective, at 19.59 hours. The Humber Super Snipe had travelled through 15 countries in 90 hours less one minute. The last 1,200 miles were covered in 24 hours, including all frontier and formality stops—an average speed of over 50 m.p.h. There remained only a routine drive of 271 miles to Lisbon to round off the trip, and for the drivers to get some well-earned sleep.

* * *

On arrival in Portugal, Stirling Moss telegraphed to Rootes: 'The car performed magnificently under dreadful conditions which made it tougher than the Monte Carlo rally.'
This was, indeed, a tribute to the Humber Super Snipe coming from such an experienced driving ace. It amply justified Rootes' optimism in planning the trial and graphically demonstrated the toughness and reliability of the Humber Super Snipe.
The owner of a Humber Super Snipe can be confident that the same qualities will serve him well in everyday service or in the most exceptional circumstances. Such a quiet, elegant, comfortable car—yet, how tough it is!

So quiet . . . So elegant . . . So comfortable

Snow, ice and hail. Freeing a mudguard of frozen snow.

The trip to Lisbon started in severe winter weather. Snow blizzards often obscured the route but did not deter Stirling Moss and his crew. Quick stops were made to free the wheels from caked, frozen snow.

Nearly there. Fixing another flag at the Portuguese frontier.

Nearing the end of their record-making trip, Stirling Moss and his crew fix the final flag to the Humber Super Snipe as they enter Portugal at Villar Formosa. They beat their own target of 5 days by 30 hours.

A typical scene. Northern Europe was covered with snow.

Wintry weather dogged the Humber Super Snipe over most of Europe. Despite adverse conditions, snow and ice-bound roads, the team continued to average 40 m.p.h. without a single stop for overhaul or repair.

London to Cape Town in 13 days 9 hrs. 6 mins.

Humber Super Snipe breaks world records—
10,500 miles over world's worst roads

At the time Stirling Moss was making his epic dash across Europe, another Humber Super Snipe was smashing the world record for London to Cape Town.

This Humber Super Snipe was also a standard model—the third off the production line and delivered to the owner only a few days before the drive.

The previous London-Cape Town record was slashed by 8 days 10 hours 39 minutes. For 10,500 miles the Humber Super Snipe was driven over the world's worst roads in 13 days 9 hours 6 minutes. Despite abnormal conditions, desert tracts, frontier delays, stops for meals and re-fuelling, the Humber Super Snipe maintained an average speed of over 32 m.p.h.—an amazing performance as any overseas motorist will readily appreciate. A remarkable tribute to the rugged stamina and sustained power of this unbeatable car.

*   *   *

The Humber Super Snipe which established the new London-Cape Town record was driven by its owner, Mr. G. C. Hinchcliffe with Mr. R. Walshaw and Mr. C. A. Longman as co-drivers.

The car left Hyde Park Corner, London, at 10.15 G.M.T. on November 26, 1952. A time schedule had been worked out. The route lay through France, Algeria, the Sahara desert, French West Africa, Nigeria, French Equatorial Africa, the Belgian Congo, North Rhodesia, South Rhodesia and so into the Union of South Africa and Cape Town. The schedule allowed for essential stops only, drivers to sleep *en route*.

Almost immediately after leaving England, the expedition met bad weather. Motoring conditions in France were appalling—blizzards, snow-storms and roads completely ice-bound. However, much worse was to come.

*   *   *

After passing through Algeria, the car arrived in the Sahara desert. This has been described as the world's worse road, but road is a courtesy title for an arid, sandy waste 2,337 miles in extent. Often the car wheels would sink into 8 or 9 inches of yielding sand. To counter the effect, the car was kept going hard at it in top and third gear, mile after mile. The drivers agree that only the sheer power and brilliant performance of the Humber Super Snipe pulled them through.

Sometimes they were forced to stop in a difficult section of the desert to lay wire netting strips for grip—an exhausting job in the glare and heat. Yet the Sahara was crossed in 75 hours 25 minutes—one of the fastest crossings ever made.

*   *   *

Following the Sahara came the rough African routes, the steaming jungles and swamps of Equatorial Africa, rivers to be forded, nightmare tracks. In these primitive conditions, the Humber Super Snipe proved its inherent toughness and forged ahead.

The windscreen had been smashed by the branch of a huge tree, paintwork had been scratched when travelling along narrow pony tracks, the body was covered with a thick layer of dust and mud. But the car itself was in fine form, running smoothly, responding immediately to all the exacting demands.

*   *   *

The arrival in Rhodesia was a relief. Here were more-civilised roads and once in South Africa the car made faster time: on the last 900 miles from Johannesburg to Cape Town, the Humber Super Snipe often exceeded 90 m.p.h. on good roads, proof that it was in good health.

*   *   *

On December 9, a cable was received: '. . . Arrived Cape Town 19.21 G.M.T., December 9. Elapsed time thirteen days nine hours six minutes. Car and crew in fine fettle.'

So ended the record-breaking trip from London to Cape Town. It proved again that the Humber Super Snipe, the quietest, the most elegant, the most comfortable of cars, can also stand up to the roughest and toughest conditions, the most gruelling tests.

So quiet . . . So elegant . . . So comfortable

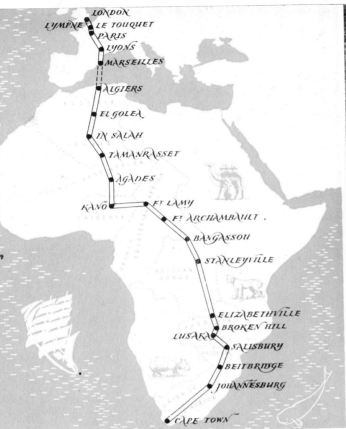

Blizzard at Lyon. A quick stop to check direction sign.

The record-making run to Cape Town also started in wintry weather. France was covered with snow storms and blizzards—roads were ice-bound. Stops were made to clean direction signs and check the destination.

In mid-Sahara. Laying wire-netting on the yielding sand.

In the Sahara, the wheels of the Humber Super Snipe would often sink 8 to 9 in. in the yielding sand. Sometimes it was necessary to lay wire netting strips for purchase— an exhausting process in that desert heat.

Across Africa. Making up time on a relatively 'good' road.

After the Sahara, came the rough African routes. These were often no more than jungle tracks through steaming jungles and across swamps. Here the Humber Super Snipe makes up time on a relatively 'good' road.

73

Triple Success

6,500 miles around Australia

All 5 Humber Super Snipes finish Reliability Trial—
Win major awards, average 50 m.p.h.

The third great success of the Humber Super Snipe was gained in the 6,500 Redex Round-Australia Reliability Trial, August, 1953.

This was the most gruelling motoring event ever organised anywhere in the world. Out of 192 starters from many countries, only 70 cars finished the rigorous course. Five production Humber Super Snipes were entered—all five checked in at the finish. They gained these major awards: 1st 2,500 c.c. and over class; 1st British car; 2nd overall, including cars of all types. In addition they received further prizes and team awards. *No other team of cars equalled this great performance.*

* * *

The object of the Australian trial was to test production models in the long winding mountain roads, flooded creeks, bog-holes, desert spaces and congested cities of Australia. Times were set for arrival at each control point with a total of 14 days for the round trip. There was less than 164 hours actual driving time, requiring an average speed of just under 50 m.p.h.

The regulations required each car to carry enough petrol and oil for a minimum of 400 miles, a gallon of water and 7 days ration for each member of the crew, a 50 ft. tow-rope, ditching gear and first-aid kit. All working parts were sealed and stamped.

* * *

The start of the 6,500-mile trek was in Sydney, the route via Brisbane and Townsville, across Queensland, north to Darwin, south through the northern territory to South Australia and Adelaide. From Adelaide it was east to Melbourne and across to Sydney again—the finishing point.

The five Humber Super Snipes entered were chosen by well-known Australian racing and competition drivers. One car was driven by the veteran racing driver Tom Sulman, another by the prominent driver Mr. Buchanan. They all praised the Snipe's reliable performance throughout the course.

At 2 p.m. on August 30, the entrants set off from Sydney. The first leg of 547 miles to Brisbane was on reasonably good roads. After 12 hours rest, there was a 500-mile drive to Rockhampton in the Queensland sugar cane country, with roads gradually deteriorating. Then another 12 hours break and a 500-mile dash to Townsville. By now, many cars had been penalised or had crashed or retired.

Then came the most gruelling test—a 670-mile race against the clock to Mount Isa, over goat tracks, corrugations, dried-up river beds. This section was strewn with wrecked or disabled cars but the five Humber Super Snipes were unscarred and the drivers again enjoyed a 12-hours rest.

* * *

From Mount Isa, the Humbers sped to Darwin, covered the 1,137 miles in the scheduled 25 hours. Sulman and Buchanan reached the half-way mark without losing a point.

The 1,000 miles from Darwin to Alice Springs, geographical centre of Australia, lay along a fine wartime highway. But the 1,100-mile dirt-track from there to Adelaide was a 'speed section'. It contained every type of hazard—sand, rock outcrops, gibber plains, rocky crossings, unbelievable dust. A breakdown here would have been serious. Yet Sulman made a record-breaking time.

* * *

The route between Adelaide and Melbourne was civilized but a 'horror section' in the 372 miles to Sydney claimed many victims. This was a course suitable for army tanks, with unbridged rivers, giant trees, sharp turns and enormous boulders. Only 17 minutes was allowed for this cross-country grind.

* * *

It is not surprising that only 70 of the 192 entrants checked in on time at Sydney: many had been abandoned 'out back'. The five successful Humber Super Snipes were no longer spick and span but in good heart. They had given final proof of the amazing endurance of this brilliant, indomitable car.

So quiet . . . So elegant . . . So comfortable

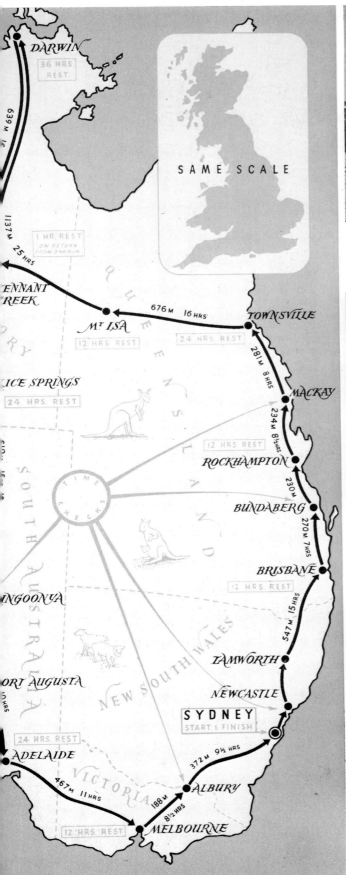

SAME SCALE

Rough going. Only tough cars survived these roads.

The 5 Humber Super Snipes entered in the Trial travelled over some of the world's roughest, dustiest routes. All 5 cars successfully finished the course.

A water jump. Rivers were forded at speed.

Every type of hazard was encountered in the 14-day trial. Sometimes flooded creeks were forded at speed. All cars were checked against fixed time schedules.

The 'horror section'. Trees, narrow tracks, hairpin bends.

The 'horror section' of the Trial claimed many victims. This was a course suitable for army tanks but all 5 Snipes survived—a great achievement for British cars.

75

Humber Pullman Mark IV from 1953. This car belonged to ex-Queen Maude of Norway, who used it as her official car.

This 1954 Pullman is probably a special or prototype. This particular bodystyle did not go into production.

exceptionally pleasant form of travel."

Several cabriolet and sedanca de ville bodies were built for the Royal tours of 1952 and 1953. These were used extensively by the Queen and the Duke of Edinburgh during their visits to Tonga, Australia and Gibraltar, together with drophead versions of the Super Snipe. The Pullmans and Imperials were again revised into their Mark IV form, with the major difference being the introduction of the 4139cc o.h.v. six-cylinder engine. This marked the end of production of the long-lived 4086cc engine that had survived since 1938.

The Super Snipes sold well, 4,397 being made in 1951. The 1952 model Super Snipe Mark IV was more advanced than it's predecessor. The Mark IV was a major re-design, with a similar chassis to the current Hawk, coil spring suspension and a new 4139cc 113 b.h.p. "Blue Riband" overhead-valve six-cylinder engine previously used in Commer trucks. This was a hugely understressed engine, the largest ever offered in a Humber, and proved very reliable, with a number of documented examples of 200,000 miles being covered before any major work was required. Automatic transmission, relatively uncommon in mid-1950s production saloons, was available as an option as well as the more common overdrive option.

Development work on the Mark IV Hawk had started

The Super Snipe Mark IVB. Note the lengthened chrome strip on the doors.

Interior of the Mark IV Super Snipe, with column gearchange and real walnut facia.

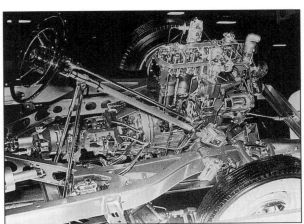

Earls Court, 1954. On the Humber stand was this magnificent 1955-season Hawk chassis with o.h.v. engine.

Mark VI Hawk.

1955 Mark VIA Hawk.

A comparitively rare 1956 Mark VI Hawk Estate car.

as early as 1949. Bill Hancock, Managing Director of the Rootes Group at that time was seen with one of the prototypes on a "proving" to Italy in tha year. The prototype is clearly identifiable as having the characteristic Hawk Mark IV body, but an elongated engine compartment, presumably to house the embryonic "Blue Riband" engine.

The Hawk was described by the late Michael Sedgwick as "..a 1942 American Sedan with British trim. It would do 95mph, but the steering was painfully low geared. The car was too big and too thirsty for British motorists, and it never caught on .."

Meanwhile, ambitious reliability trials for the Super Snipe were staged by the publicity department, where on one, Stirling Moss, Leslie Johnson, John Cutts and works mechanic David Humphrey and a Humber Super Snipe were sent on a 3,332-mile trip in December

Gordon Motors, one of Queensland's Rootes agents. This 1954 picture shows a Mark V Hillman Minx, a Mark IVA Super Snipe and a Mark III Super Snipe lined up on the garage forecourt.

Mark IV Humber Super Snipe at the 1954 Monte Carlo Rally. Raymond Baxter is in the passenger seat recording an interview for the B.B.C.

1952 from Norway to Portugal to demonstrate the *"stamina, speed and "driveability" of the new Humber Super Snipe"*. The purpose of this was to popularise the Humber Super Snipe, and every effort was made to ensure that the event was covered by the press, who were flown to key locations during the course of the trial.

Averaging a speed of 40 m.p.h., the Super Snipe arrived in Portugal 24 hours ahead of schedule. Norman Garrad, recalling the preparations for the attempt, had originally intended that the attempt would commence from Lisbon and finish in Oslo. However, William Rootes beleived that the attempt would stand more chance of success if commencing in the north. A number of arrangements were made for the crossing of the 15 frontiers involved and, in Switzerland, the arrival of the car was carefully timed to coincide with the clearing of snow in a particularly difficult pass. Here, the driver of the plough was asked to proceed up the run with the car following immediately afterwards.

A second Mark IV Super Snipe was sent on a record breaking endurance trial from London to Cape Town over some of the world's worst roads. George Hinchcliff, Robbie Walsaw and Charles Longman did attempt to better their first record of 13 days 9 hours and six minutes by attempting the return journey, but despite being ahead of schedule they were forced to retire with a holed sump in the Sahara desert. Rootes supplied the car to Hinchcliffe and subsequently recovered it from the Sahara. Once back in the UK in its battered state, it was sent on promotional trips around the UK Humber dealers and distributors.

A third trip was organised to Australia in August 1953, when a Super Snipe was entered in the 6,500 mile Redex Reliability Trial. The car averaged 50 m.p.h. throughout and gained awards in three classes.

However, the Super Snipe did not prove to be a success in the 1953 Monte Carlo Rally, the car driven by Goff Imhoff crashing in the Alps.

Several improvements to the fittings and trim were made to the Super Snipe Mark III, with modifications to the rear bench seats to provide comfortable accommodation for three and the use of burr walnut on the facia and the door cappings, an attempt was made to move the Super Snipe up-market.

In October 1955, on the Super Snipe Mark IVA, overdrive was offered as an optional extra, with the engine power increased to 116 b.h.p., brakes enlarged, steering lightened and the irritating automatic choke, which could pull the car along at over 20 m.p.h. in top, replaced by a conventional manual choke. Externally, a chrome strip under the side windows was added and a pressed-in number plate holder was fitted on the boot lid. Automatic transmission became an option for the first time in April 1956 on the Mark IVB, and the engine was uprated to 122 b.h.p. from 116 b.h.p., Sales had levelled off at 2,000 per year and this Super Snipe was phased out for the 1957 season.

One or two large six-light metal estate cars were used by the B.B.C. in 1953 and other variants included several hundred pick-up truck conversions for the Kuwait Oil Company, also numerous chassis were made available for the mounting of hearse and ambulance bodies by specialist coachbuilders.

The Humber Hawk Mark V, introduced in late 1952, fitted with the 2267 side-valve unit, was immediately distinguishable from the Hawk Mark IV by the lowered bonnet line. There was revised front-end styling, with new side and centre grilles and new bumpers with overriders. Improvements were made to the handling by fitting bigger dampers on the back and firmer setting on the front suspension.

In June 1954 came the introduction of the last of the separate-chassis Humber Hawks, the Mark VI. The 2.3 litre engine acquired overhead valves and the power was increased from 58 to 70 b.h.p., resulting in a car capable of over 80 m.p.h. and having a 0-50 acceleration time of only 15 seconds. The same engine was used in the Sunbeam Talbot 90s which enjoyed rallying success driven by Stirling Moss and Sheila Van Damm. With bigger brakes and better handling, the car was identifiable by longer, square cut rear wings and the use of a chrome strip along the front wing and door instead of along the sill below the doors.

An estate car was added to the civilian range for the first time. This had squared-off rear panelling in which was set a horizontally split rear tailgate. This featured a wind-down rear window into the tailgate before it could be released and pulled down to form the loading platform. The rear bench seat folded flat to take extra luggage. One of these estate cars was delivered to Winston Churchill, who already owned a Pullman IV limousine.

7. THE SERIES CARS

The Series cars were a departure for the Humber company. Many variations were built, and in common with American practice, some change or other was announced for each motor show, which resulted in a proliferation of different series over the ten years they were in production. Some were merely minor modifications to the specification, but, particulary in the early years of the series, efforts were continually made to improve the basic mechanical specification.

During the early 1950s, the Rootes board had considered the extensive investment necessary to introduce new cars into the group. Modern automobile design was moving away from the separate chassis and body idea to one of unitary or monocoque construction. 1955 had seen the launch of the Series I Sunbeam Rapier, a sports coupe and in 1956 the "new" Hillman Minx. It thus fell to Ted Knight, Chief Stylist and Engineering Director Bernard "B.B" Winter to develop the "new" Hawk/Super Snipe family on the same principle.

In 1955 and 1956, *Airflow Streamline Limited* of Northampton build prototypes of the bodyshells for the Hawk/Super Snipe as a common body was to be used for both. As test engineers, they were commissioned to carry out the development work in conjunction with Humber's design team.

The Hawk was released to the public in May 1957 with single and dual-tone paint options. It was powered by Humber's four-cylinder 2267cc 78 b.h.p. overhead-valve engine, carried over from the Mark VI, itself a development of the earlier side-valve unit. The distributor was moved to the front and lower down on the engine to be driven off a skew gear from the camshaft. The idea was to achieve a low bonnet-line. The front suspension was now mounted on a sub-frame with unequal length wishbones, coil springs and vertical dampers. The assembly bolted onto the chassis rails on rubber mountings to reduce vibration.

Laycock Overdrive was available as an option, as was Borg-Warner DG-type automatic transmission. Body panels were pressed and supplied by *British Light Steel Pressings* of Acton, London, (a wholly owned Rootes subsidiary), and then assembled at the Ryton factory. These bodyshells were the largest built at the time in Britain. The new bodies had a wrap-around windscreen and rear window and more cabin space. Externally, the styling of the series Humbers was clearly influenced by mid-1950s American saloons, and the early series cars resemble the 1955 Chevrolet two-ten series. There was a low, wide grille with horizontal bars flanked by cowled headlamps and rectangular sidelamps. In the cabin, leather bench seats with folding central armrests were fitted giving seating for six persons. A new "wood-effect" metal dash was included, but "real" walnut veneer was used on the door-trim. A heater was an optional extra, though, a strange idiosyncracy for a luxury car. An unusual petrol filler cap was incorporated in the offside rear lamp reflector, following contemporary American practice. This caught out many a petrol pump attendant!

Detailed photograph of the cabin of one of the prototype "Series" cars. These were wider than the previous "Mark" cars and included a re-working of the interior appointments. This incorporated a padded dash for the first time and spacious accommodation for six adults.

Prototype Series Humber "Snipe". This was Humber's first monocoque design and incorporated a number of transatlantic influences. The detail shows the petrol filler cap incorporated in the circular reflector of the rear light cluster and the full-width treatment of the radiator grille.

A Touring Limousine was also offered, with the only major difference being the separation of the front and rear compartments by a wind-down glass partition.

Two weeks after it's launch, the car was awarded the grand prize of honour by the *Automobile Club of Italy* in their *International Elegance Competition* in Rome. The car was judged against contemporary cars around the world. As usual, the Rootes publicity machine made the most of this in it's advertising and public relations campaigns.

In October 1957, an estate car was added to the range. This was mechanically identical to the saloon car, but an interesting innovation, being one of the very few luxury production estate cars then available. Once more, American influence was brought to bear on the design and from the rear the car had overtones of the 1956 Chevrolet Nomad Station Wagon, with curved in side windows, a horizontally split tailgate featuring an upper glazed unit which hinged upwards and a lower steel panel, released by an internal lever, which when pulled down was held horizontal by steel cables at each side. When lowered the tailgate could then be used as a loading platform. The number plate unit remained

vertical throughout the operation. A lift-up load area panel allowed access to the spare wheel, jack and tools. The Estate cars were later assembled by *Carbodies of Coventry,* who are now better known for the Austin FX4 London Taxi.

Prices were initially £840 for the saloon and £920 for the Touring Limousine and the Estate was priced at £1,160.

Reviewing the Humber Hawk in June 1957, T*he Autocar* remarked that:

"Few entirely new production models have passed a full test with more honour. In the market for which it is intended the car will win wide respect - and quickly - for its appearance, accommodation, comfort and quality. It is economical to run and, not least moderately priced."

The series Hawk began to be updated and a number of minor changes were made to the model. These included the addition of a larger 12.5 gallon fuel tank from 11.5 gallons introduced late in 1957 and a restyled walnut facia to replace the original metal dash. In October 1958, another re-vamp took place, with a heater at last becoming standard and an internal bonnet

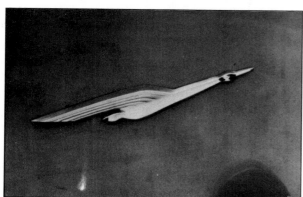

This is a second prototype vehicle, which was badged as a "Super Snipe" on the off-side and "Hawk" on the near-side. Note the different treatment of the flash along each side of the vehicle and additional trim which did not appear on the production vehicle. The engine on this prototype is a four-cylinder o.h.v. unit which had been fitted in the Mark VI Hawk. The interior is from a different car, with a dash-mounted rear-view mirror and a Snipe Mascot on the bonnet.

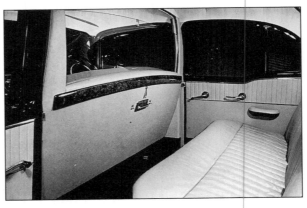

Early production Series Hawk. These contemporary Rootes publicity photographs demonstrate the spaciousness of the accommodation and the load carrying capacity. Note the cleaner treatment of the front radiator grille and the fashionable two-tone paint scheme. Although appearing to be genuine from these shots the dash was a metal wood-effect affair that did not prove popular and was replaced half-way through the production of the Series I Hawk. The picture with the bonnet open is supposed to demonstrate ease of servicing. These saloons were also available with a limousine division.

Floorpan for the Humber Hawk, shown in the press shop at the Acton plant.

The Humber Hawk assembly line. The body was held in a jig whilst a sequence of welding operations was carried out.

Humber Hawk assembly line. This photo, from contemporary Rootes publicity material, was heavily retouched!

Testing of a Hawk under extreme weather conditions.

release being provided below the facia, as the early cars had an externally-released bonnet. The Series IA Hawk was introduced in October 1959 and featured different gear ratios and a full length side flash, but was otherwise identical to the Series I.

In October 1958, the Super Snipe was re-launched, using the same bodyshell as the Hawk but with number of changes to accommodate the all-new six-cylinder 2651cc overhead-valve 118b.h.p. engine, designed in conjunction with Armstrong-Siddeley.

Armstrong-Siddeley's car making business was only a small part of the Bristol-Siddeley aero-engine and aircraft company. Armstrong Siddeley were commissioned to jointly produce a new engine to replace the Commer engine of the Super Snipe Mark IV. This was a shrewd move. Armstrong Siddeley already had a suitable engine, a 3.4 litre "six" in their Sapphire model, and the design was broadly based on this. Although the new engine was to be along the lines of the 3.4 litre Sapphire unit in layout, it would be an all-new undertaking. By the autumn of 1958, running a year

late, the new engine was ready and was a marked departure from traditional Humber engineering. For the first time the stroke was reduced to equal the bore dimension. Two-thirds of the size of the "Blue Riband" engine, it produced almost the same power. Advanced features included hemispherical combustion chambers within a cross-flow cylinder-head and twin rocker shafts.

Originally intended to be introduced at the same time as the Hawk, this had been prevented by the delays in developing the engine. Nevertheless, this was the most luxuriously equipped car made by the Rootes group and was initially available, as was the Hawk, in three versions, the four-door saloon, a touring limousine and an estate car. The standard equipment included a three-speed all-syncromesh gearbox with column gearchange and power steering as an optional extra. Other options were overdrive and automatic transmission. Externally, there was an egg-crate-like front grille featuring five horizontal bars with wrap-around surrounds which incorporated rectangular sidelights. Inside, bench seats could accommodate six people in comfort and two folding tables were built into the front seat squab. Leather upholstery, pile carpets and walnut finish on door cappings, facia and folding tables completed the picture. The Reutter front seat with integral armrests was also an option. A Snipe bird mascot adorned the bonnet mounted on a plinth and the name H U M B E R was incorporated within a chrome

Production Series I Super Snipe powered by a six-cylinder 112 b.h.p. 2.6 litre engine.

This diagram contrasts the profile of the Mark VI Hawk and a Series car. This demonstrates how the designers were able to extend the interior cabin dimensions without any significant increase in the overall length of the car.

moulding on the leading edge. Like the Hawk touring limousine, the Super Snipe was designed for chauffeur driving, with a wind-down partition between the front and rear compartments. Similarly, the estate was mechanically identical to the saloon.

Again, this new Humber was well received. *The Motor* commented that:

"Both to buy and to run, it is a car which many successful business and professional people will regard as anything but extravagantly expensive, its merits as either a chauffeur-driven or owner-driven car being great for smooth travel around town or for rapid progress in open country."

William Boddy of *Motor Sport* remarked:

*"I am pleased to find the old name of Humber associated with a car which is not only very fully and sensibly equipped but which posseses ample performance. This Super Snipe, which runs so smoothly and silently by grace of the excellent new engine with the ingenious valve-gear, represents first class travel which should appeal particularly to successful busi-*nessmen."*

Some limousine conversions were carried out by Harold Radford of Hammersmith, West London, who later added a countryman version featuring split rear seats, full-length sun-roof, plus a host of extras for picnics and outdoor events. This added up to £850, more than half the original purchase price of the car!

The first modifications to the Super Snipe Series cars were made in October 1959 when the Series II model adopted disc brakes and different gear ratios. A stiffer antiroll bar was added and the suspension upgraded, but the greatest change was the introduction of the uprated 2965cc six-cylinder, 129 b.h.p. engine which was capable of taking the car to a maximum speed of over 95 m.p.h. The front egg-crate grille was revised to incorporate four horizontal grille bars and separate H U M B E R letters across the front of the bonnet.

In October 1960, the Series II Hawk was introduced, featuring servo-assisted disc brakes, larger rear drums, redesigned rear suspension and an improved four-speed gearbox. In the interior, seats were redesigned, which meant a change from traditional leather to a PVC material, and a heater, ammeter, oil pressure gauge and windscreen washers were added to the standard equipment.

Around this time, various styling exercises were undertaken to revamp the front-end design of the car. With the launch of the Series III Super Snipe with its radically altered front which now featured twin headlamps, it was thought that the Hawk ought to be given some updating as well. Several artist's impressions have been seen showing revised radiator grilles ranging from what can only be described as a late 1950s Morris Isis look to a Mark I Ford Cortina-style grille with extensive use of pressed aluminium. However, these schemes came to nothing and the front end of the Hawk remained virtually unchanged until the model's demise in 1967.

The Series I Super Snipe Estate interior. Here the rear seats are folded down to increase the load-carrying capacity.

The Series III Hawk cars, introduced in September 1962, featured more elaborate modifications to the Series II, such as an improved steering gear unit, to meet criticisms about the model's heavy steering, the increase in the fuel tank capacity from 12½ to 16 gallons. Inside, driver and passenger comfort was enhanced by the addition of an improved heating and ventilation system and the external appearance of the car was modified by the restyling of the rear window and windscreen surrounds on the saloon and Touring Limousine. Series III cars had chrome trim along the gutters which continued down to the tops of the rear wings.

Similarly, in October 1960, the Humber Super Snipe Series III was also introduced. Improvements in the suspension and steering had been made to correct the Series II's tyre scrubbing on tight corners and it's tendency to understeer. However, most of the modifications were to the external appearance of the model, the Super Snipe now being the first British production car to feature dual headlamps together with flashing indica-tors alongside the sidelamps and a restyled horizontal grille with horizontal bars. The Snipe mascot was removed for safety reasons and a modified side trim was fitted.

Although an "executive" car, the Super Snipe did enjoy some success in the 1961 RAC Rally in the over 1600cc class in Series Production cars. Driven by Raymond Baxter of the B.B.C., together with Leonard Millar, a Super Snipe gained a first in its class to add to the team prizes won by the other Rootes entrants, the Sunbeam Rapiers. Three Super Snipes were to com-pete in the gruelling four-day East African Safari Rally in 1962, and in 1963 Peter Harper was again entered in the over 1600cc class in a Humber Super Snipe.

September 1962 saw the introduction of the Super Snipe Series IV, which featured similar bodywork change as the Series III Hawk, but the rear doors incorporated opening quarter lights and a new badge was fitted in the centre of the grille, with the snipe bird motif and the legend "Rootes Group". The steering gear was once

Series I Hawk Estate. Released at the same time as the saloon, this was one of the very few estate versions of a luxury saloon which was available at that time. The picture at the top of the page is of the Humber stand at the 1957 Motor Show. The second picture is of the display at the Rootes showrooms at Devonshire House, Piccadilly, featuring the Estate and the saloon. These are very clearly early estate cars which feature a number plate mounted below the tailgate and illuminated by a bulb within the chrome bumber. This was subsequently dropped and a more conventional mounting fitted to the tailgate.

more modified and transmission improved with the addition of a new diaphragm clutch. Like the Hawk, fuel capacity was increased to 16 gallons and the driver was given additional warning lights which indicated when fuel reserves had fallen below two gallons, when the brake fluid level was low and when the handbrake was on. The horsepower rating of the engine was increased from 129 b.h.p. to 132.5 b.h.p. by increasing inlet valve size and the rear axle ratio was changed from 4.55:1 to 4.22:1.

Peter Ware, Rootes Engineering Director from 1950 to 1965, relates an interesting story concerning the design of the engine. To reduce weight and "rumble" at

Series I Super Snipe Estate. Not as common as the Hawk, fewer were produced and only a handful survive today.

Taken in Victoria, Australia in 1957, this photograph is of Reginald Rootes with the "new" Series I Hawk and a 1913 Humberette.

high revs, manufacturing the block in light alloy and mounting the shaft on seven bearings instead of five was considered. The aim was to emulate the engineering excellence of the Mercedes 220 saloon, one of which was kept by the Humber department as a "stalking horse". However, lack of finance meant that these proposals were not taken up.

Looking to the future development of the model during 1964, and the possible replacement of the Series cars with a new model, the engineering department was given a Chrysler Valiant for technical analysis to determine whether improvements could be made at the production engineering stage. A detailed report was prepared on the car's construction, even down to the moulding clips. However the project was again shelved through lack of finance. It is ironic that when Series car production finally ceased in 1967 it was the Chrysler Valiant which was then offered as an alternative.

October 1964 saw some more substantial improvements to the Super Snipe, now redesignated Series V. A new restyled, flatter roofline was incorporated, a feature that was included across the whole Rootes range. The model featured hinged rear quarter lights separated from the doors. Performance was improved by the introduction of twin side-draft Stromberg CD-

This Series I Super Snipe was used as a prop for this 1964 publicity shot for the Beatles.

175 carburettors and a new manifold. This resulted in the first genuine 100 m.p.h. production Humber. A Lucas alternator replaced the dynamo, though the Hawks continued with the dynamo until the end of production. The exhaust system was modified and improved with the introduction of extra silencers. A simplified, redesigned facia was incorporated together with improvements to the gearchange. New bumpers with overriders incorporating rubber facings and restyled auxilliary lighting front and rear identified the new

Rootes development engineers put the 1960 Series II Hawk through it's paces at MIRA.

Series II Super Snipe Police-specification Estate, featuring the larger 2965 cc six-cylinder engine. These were popular with motorway patrols and were amongst the first police cars to cover the M1 motorway. The interior shot shows some of the comprehensive equipment which was easily accommodated in rear cabin. Each Police force had different requirements which could be dealt with by local Rootes dealers.

model. The Estate car's bodywork was unaltered, the cost of re-engineering for a limited production run being considered unjustifiable.

At the same time, the Imperial name was revived for the first time since 1954. Effectively a very high specification Super Snipe, featuring as standard a PVC leathercloth roof covering, Borg-Warner DG-type automatic transmission, power-assisted steering and "Select-a-ride", electrically adjustable rear dampers, which were controlled from a four-position rotary switch under the dashboard. West of England cloth upholstery was an alternative to leather, and the separate front seats had Reutter fully-reclining squabs with drop-leaf tables behind. Separate controlled heating systems for front and rear compartments were fitted, as well as individual reading lamps for rear passengers, who could then easily read the *Financial Times* without distracting the chauffeur. Radio and external fog and spot-lamps completed the luxury specification and the Imperial was available either as a saloon or limousine.

The bodies were trimmed by Thrupp & Maberly of Cricklewood, North London, whose nameplate was fitted on the sills. With a top speed of between 97 and 100 m.p.h., this was a car which compared well with the best of the day's luxury saloons. It was cheaper than the Daimler Majestic Major at £2,703 in Britain, and compared well the American Rambler 770 Six at £1,861 and Studebaker Commander at £1,918, which, though well-equipped, were not really in the luxury car class. Only Jaguar, with the Mark II 3.8 and Rover P5 3-litre were of a comparable price and quality, but the Jaguar was less spacious and the Rover's roadholding

The Autocar, 21 October 1960

This somewhat inaccurate artist's impression is how the British public first saw the Series III Super Snipe.

1960 Series II Hawk Saloon. Very few external changes were made apart from the new side flash.

1961 advertising for the Series III Super Snipe. This included a revised front end, with the first example of double headlamps on a British production car.

1961 Series III Police specification Super Snipe.

and braking inferior to the Humber.

At the same time, the Hawk Series IV underwent similar body styling changes as the Super Snipe with the upper cabin substantially modified, an enlarged glass area, a flatter rear window and the addition of a rear fixed quarter light.

The Series cars were exported around the world either fully built-up or C.K.D. (completely knocked down) for reassembly. Rootes had factories in Melbourne, Australia and Wellington, New Zealand for the re-assembly of C.K.D.s. The vaguaries of the New Zealand market resulted in some Hillmans being converted to Humbers by "badge-engineering" the Mark and Series Hillman Minxes in the 1960s.

In Australia, the Chrysler Valiant range, consisting of the Chrysler Valiant Regal Saloon with a six-cylinder 4.3

U.S. versions of the Series III Super Snipe were equipped with air conditioning units fitted below the main facia. This was powered by a belt-driven compressor fitted to the side of the engine.

Series IV Super Snipe saloon. Introduced in 1962, this can be identified by the badge on the grille with the legend "Rootes Group" on the grille badge, which also featured the traditional Snipe bird motif. The saloons had opening rear-door quarterlights and restyled rear windows.

Series IV Super Snipe Ambulance conversions were fitted to the Series III, IV and V, with a glass reinforced plastic bodyshell. These were built at Geelong, Victoria by the Australian Government Aircraft Corporation and served mainly in Victoria and Tasmania.

Series III Hawk saloons from 1962. This photo of the Coventry Police fleet was taken in 1964.

Series IV Super Snipe Estate car.

litre engine, the Valient CH Saloon, the Valiant Regal Estate and the Valiant Charger Coupe, all powered by a V8 engine, were offered alongside the Rootes vehicles, following an acquisition of a stake in the Rootes group by Chrysler. These were all imported into the UK and were offered as Humber substitutes following the phasing out of the Hawk and the Super Snipe in 1967. The Valiant could well have been the basis of the new Hawk/Super Snipe family, but marketing and engineering resources were directed towards the development of the new "Arrow" cars, which, using one basic bodyshell, were intended to provide a replacement for many of the outdated Rootes cars.

The big Humbers were popular with police forces throughout the country, as well as government departments and the funeral and carriage trades. Woodhall-Nicholson and Colman-Milne produced "stretched" versions of the Hawk and Super Snipe which featured tip-up occasional seats in the rear compartment, which could then accommodate up to five passengers.

Humber Super Snipes also featured in rallies in Europe and Africa, as well as closer to home in the RAC rallies. Drivers included Peter Harper and Raymond Baxter.

At the end of production, a nationwide price-cutting exercise was undertaken to reduce stocks of Hawks, Super Snipes and Imperials as quickly as possible with over £200 being taken off the list prices. A shabby end

Series IV Super Snipe stretched Limousine conversion, believed to be by Colman-Milne.

Series IV Super Snipe Hearse conversion by Woodall Nicholson Limited of Halifax.

was fully carpeted and the four doors each had courtesy lights. *Motor Sport* commented that:

".. the Humber Sceptre will become deservedly popular and the astonishing fact remains that the Rootes Group somehow contrives to sell its latest Humber model for only £997.8s.9d inclusive of purchase tax. The basic price is but £825 and remembering how the £ has depreciated since the war this is a remarkable figure for such a good, well turned-out, high performance family car."

By 1965, the Sceptre was due for a facelift and in the autumn, the Humber Sceptre Mark II was released. Powered by the Rootes five-bearing 1,725cc engine, and provided with Borg-Warner automatic transmission as an option, the car was also significantly changed in its external appearance. The front end was reworked so that the same nose as the Hillman Minx was used, but with a different grille and a four-headlamp design.

However, by 1964, the Humber range was beginning to become dated, especially in terms of performance, and with capital already tied up in the costly Imp project and the serious dispute at British Light Steel

for a once noble car.

At the beginning of 1963, Humber announced a small "entry model", the Humber Sceptre. This was meant to bridge the gap between the Hillman and Humber ranges by providing a small luxury car, and was a combination of features from several of the Rootes ranges. The radiator grille was pure Sunbeam Rapier and much of the development work on the prototype was done with a view to introducing a Series IV Sunbeam Rapier, and certainly photographs of the prototypes confirm this. However, it is possible that the car may have been deliberately badged as a Humber to compete with the newly released up-market Rover 2000.

The Sceptre was powered by a 1,592cc push-rod, four-cylinder o.h.v. engine with twin Zenith carbutettors. Coupled to a four-speed gearbox, with syncromesh in 2nd, 3rd and top, together with Laycock de Normanville overdrive, the Sceptre was a fast car for its day and had a maximum speed of around 90 m.p.h. and an overall fuel consumption of 23 m.p.g. The body lines were built around a sharply-curved windscreen with well-raked side pillars and a low roof-line. The interior was somewhat disappointing, with p.v.c. upholstery instead of leather and an anti dazzle black facia instead of the traditional walnut. However, the car was well-equipped, a heater was standard, anti dazzle visors contained vanity mirrors, reversing lamps were included, the floor

Series IV Hawk development car pictured here on test in mid-Wales. Note the Series III rear light clusters and bumpers.

Carriages at Midnight...

The Humber Super Snipe glides effortlessly and naturally into the most gracious way of life. Stately in its comfort, it offers you the luxury of English hide upholstery and styling at a truly aristocratic level. With a 6-cylinder, 3-litre engine, power-assisted steering, sure braking that includes front discs and top speed of 100 m.p.h., the Humber Super Snipe gives you that Lord-of-the-Manor feeling every time you settle behind the wheel. Discover the feeling for yourself by arranging a test drive with your Humber dealer.

*£1,572.7.11 inc. £272.7.11 p.t., in a range of distinguished colours. Overdrive, fully-automatic transmission and wing mirrors available as extras. Also available Humber Imperial *£1,892.12.1 inc. £327.12.1 p.t. and Humber Hawk *£1,161.11.3 inc. £201.11.3 p.t. *Recommended prices.

BY APPOINTMENT TO
HER MAJESTY THE QUEEN
MOTOR VEHICLE
MANUFACTURERS
ROOTES MOTORS LIMITED

ROOTES
MOTORS LIMITED

LONDON SHOWROOMS AND EXPORT DIVISION · DEVONSHIRE HOUSE · PICCADILLY · LONDON W1

HUMBER SUPER SNIPE

Series V Super Snipe advertisement from Country Life.

Series IV Hawk. A number of new features can be seen here. The most obvious is the squared roof-line and the modified treatment of the panels and windows from the waist up. Other changes included the new bumpers with rubber-faced over-riders and the larger rear reflectors, which, like a similar modification on the Series V Super Snipe, were changed back to the original fairly early in the production run. The front auxilliary lamp cluster now included the coloured indicators. Inside the dash was again revised using new instruments. Improvements were made to the column gearchange.

The October 1964 Motor Show saw the introduction of the new Humber Imperial, resurrecting a model name unused since 1953. The mechanical specification was the same as the Super Snipe, but without manual option and with a higher standard of interior appointments.

1966 Series V Super Snipe Estate. The Estate versions of the Series V Super Snipe and Series IV Hawk still retained the body panels and roofline from the earlier models. The front end styling was the same as the saloons, as was the treatment of the bumpers and the front and rear lights.

Limousine version of the Series V Super Snipe with glass division between front and rear compartments. Later cars had two sliding glass panels.

The Sunday Express of 2nd January 1966 carried this short item on Prime Ministerial motoring preferences!

Pressings in recent years, the company was looking for a relatively cheap way of updating the range, as the design exercises previously carried out could not be financially justified. Having demonstrated to the Rootes board that dramatic improvements in the Sunbeam Alpine range had been brought about by the installation of an American Ford V8 engine, this appeared to be a simple solution to the problem of enhancing the performance of the Humber at a modest cost and improving the specification to compete on equal terms with cars such as the more expensive 120 m.p.h. Daimler Majestic Major, which was powered by a 4.5 litre V8 engine. It was known that Rover was dabbling with a Buick-designed V8 to fit to their P5 range and, in 1964, the Rootes board asked the Product Planning department which of the Rootes range was a most suitable candidate for the fitting of a V8 engine. The models suggested were the Humber Sceptre and the Humber Super Snipe, together with the top-of-the-range Humber Imperial. With the investment made by Chrysler, it was them, rather than to Ford, that the engineers looked to for a suitable engine.

For the Humber Sceptre, the unit chosen was the 4.4 litre engine as fitted to the Chrysler "Barracuda".

The V8 Super Snipe. These rare photographs of the prototype show the proposed badging and the comparitively tight fit of the Chrysler engine in the Super Snipe engine bay. A third photograph shows the engine out of the car with the specially made exhaust manifolds which enabled the unit to be "shoehorned" into the bodyshell.

Below are the comparative performance figures for the Super Snipe and the V8 recorded by the test engineers in 1966. The overall performance of the V8 was only a marginal improvement on the straight six, with a noticeable deterioration in fuel consumption.

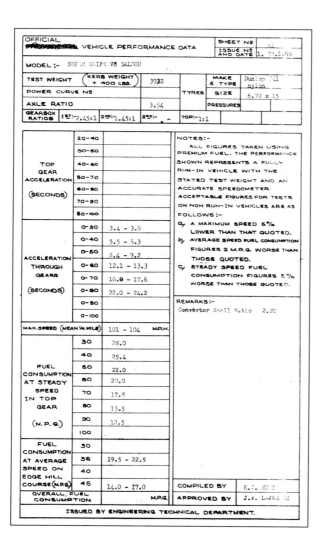

OFFICIAL ~~PROVISIONAL~~ VEHICLE PERFORMANCE DATA

		SHEET Nº	44
		ISSUE Nº AND DATE	1. 28.1.66

MODEL :- SUPER SNIPE V8 SALOON

TEST WEIGHT (KERB WEIGHT + 400 LBS.)	3932		MAKE & TYPE	Dunlop C41 nylon
POWER CURVE Nº		TYRES	SIZE	6.70 x 15
AXLE RATIO	3.54		PRESSURES	
GEARBOX RATIOS 1ST:-2.45:1 2ND:-1.45:1 3RD:- - TOP:-1:1				

			NOTES:-
TOP GEAR ACCELERATION (SECONDS)	20-40		ALL FIGURES TAKEN USING PREMIUM FUEL. THE PERFORMANCE SHOWN REPRESENTS A FULLY RUN-IN VEHICLE WITH THE STATED TEST WEIGHT AND AN ACCURATE SPEEDOMETER. ACCEPTABLE FIGURES FOR TESTS ON NON RUN-IN VEHICLES ARE AS FOLLOWS:-
	30-50		
	40-60		
	50-70		
	60-80		
	70-90		
	80-100		
ACCELERATION THROUGH GEARS (SECONDS)	0-30	3.4 - 3.9	a) A MAXIMUM SPEED 5% LOWER THAN THAT QUOTED.
	0-40	5.5 - 6.3	b) AVERAGE SPEED FUEL CONSUMPTION FIGURES 2 M.P.G. WORSE THAN THOSE QUOTED.
	0-50	8.4 - 9.2	
	0-60	12.1 - 13.3	c) STEADY SPEED FUEL CONSUMPTION FIGURES 5% WORSE THAN THOSE QUOTED.
	0-70	16.8 - 17.6	
	0-80	22.0 - 24.2	
	0-90		
	0-100		REMARKS:-
MAX.SPEED (MEAN ¼ MILE)		101 - 104 M.P.H.	Converter Stall Ratio 2.20
FUEL CONSUMPTION AT STEADY SPEED IN TOP GEAR (M.P.G.)	30	28.0	
	40	25.4	
	50	22.0	
	60	20.0	
	70	17.8	
	80	15.5	
	90	12.5	
	100		
FUEL CONSUMPTION AT AVERAGE SPEED ON EDGE HILL COURSE (M.P.G)	30		
	36	19.5 - 22.5	
	40		
	45	14.0 - 17.0	COMPILED BY R.J. HUNT
OVERALL FUEL CONSUMPTION		M.P.G.	APPROVED BY J.A. LAWRENCE

ISSUED BY ENGINEERING TECHNICAL DEPARTMENT.

OFFICIAL ~~PROVISIONAL~~ VEHICLE PERFORMANCE DATA

		SHEET Nº	41
		ISSUE Nº AND DATE	1 (6.5.66.)

MODEL :- SUPER SNIPE V OVERDRIVE (7.5 : 1 C.r.)

TEST WEIGHT (KERB WEIGHT + 400 LBS.)	3972		MAKE & TYPE	DUNLOP C41N
POWER CURVE Nº	184	TYRES	SIZE	6.70 x 15
AXLE RATIO	4.22		PRESSURES F27 R27	
GEARBOX RATIOS 1ST:- 2.803 2ND:-1.452 3RD:- - TOP:- 1.0 O/D TOP .778 REV. 1.137				

			NOTES:-
TOP GEAR ACCELERATION (SECONDS)	20-40	8.7 - 9.7	ALL FIGURES TAKEN USING PREMIUM FUEL. THE PERFORMANCE SHOWN REPRESENTS A FULLY RUN-IN VEHICLE WITH THE STATED TEST WEIGHT AND AN ACCURATE SPEEDOMETER. ACCEPTABLE FIGURES FOR TESTS ON NON RUN-IN VEHICLES ARE AS FOLLOWS:-
	30-50	9.1 - 10.1	
	40-60	9.8 - 10.8	
	50-70	11.3 - 12.4	
	60-80	14.4 - 15.8	
	70-90		
	80-100		
ACCELERATION THROUGH GEARS (SECONDS)	0-30	5.0 - 6.0	a) A MAXIMUM SPEED 5% LOWER THAN THAT QUOTED.
	0-40	8.5 - 9.5	b) AVERAGE SPEED FUEL CONSUMPTION FIGURES 2 M.P.G. WORSE THAN THOSE QUOTED.
	0-50	11.5 - 12.6	
	0-60	15.6 - 17.2	c) STEADY SPEED FUEL CONSUMPTION FIGURES 5% WORSE THAN THOSE QUOTED.
	0-70	21.8 - 24.0	
	0-80		
	0-90		REMARKS:-
	0-100		See Sheet 21 for Direct Drive Top Gear Steady Speed Fuel Consumptions.
MAX.SPEED (MEAN ¼ MILE)		97 - 100 M.P.H.	
FUEL CONSUMPTION AT STEADY SPEED IN TOP GEAR (M.P.G.)	30	(26.8	* TYRE PRESSURE USED BY EXPERIMENTAL FOR THIS TEST.
	40	(25.9	
	50	24.2	
	60	23.0	
	70	20.8	
	80	18.1	
	90		
	100		
FUEL CONSUMPTION AT AVERAGE SPEED ON EDGE HILL COURSE (M.P.G)	30		
	36	22 - 25	
	40	20 - 23	
	45		COMPILED BY Chris Wright
OVERALL FUEL CONSUMPTION		M.P.G.	APPROVED BY J. Lawrence

ISSUED BY ENGINEERING TECHNICAL DEPARTMENT.

1967 saw the end of production of the Series cars and drastic reductions in price in order to clear stocks.

This was a powerful V8 with a compression ratio of 10.5:1 and a 4-barrel Holley carburettor, which developed 196 b.h.p. at 5100 r.p.m. Brakes and suspension were uprated to those fitted in the Mark II Sunbeam Tiger, and Torqueflight automatic transmission provided the drive via a 3.07:1 Salisbury differential.

The V8 Sceptre was a Mark II Hillman Minx with a Sceptre grille. However, despite the excellent 133 m.p.h. performance, the fastest ever by a Humber, the car was only capable of being offered as an automatic and the location of the engine forward in the chassis frame made the steering unacceptably heavy. Because of necessary modification to the bulkhead to allow the fitting of the V8, there was a serious amount of intrusion to front passenger space in the cabin. The prototype car underwent several years of development, but was eventually broken up by Chrysler.

Nevertheless the Vehicle Development Department was given the go-ahead to draw up plans to offer the V8 as an option on the Humber Super Snipe and Imperial. A project intention circular issued on 18th October 1965 indicated that apart from the fitting of the Chrysler 273 c.u. B2 Series V8 with 2-barrel carburettor, a number of other refinements were to be added at a later stage. Intermittent windscreen wipers, an automatic dipping mirror, electrically operated windows, a Lucas cruise control unit and a redesigned air-conditioning unit

to be offered as part of the standard specification. Transmission was to be the Chrysler "Torqueflite" automatic three-speed type 904.

Six prototype cars were planned, code-named SC (Snipe-Chrysler). More than sufficient space was found in the engine bay of the first prototype, SC1, a silver-grey Super Snipe, and after modifying the engine mountings a 312 c.u. four-barrel V8 was fitted together with a manual transmission. The car was then fitted with a Salisbury differential and sent for testing at MIRA where a maximum speed of 125 m.p.h. was achieved at a cost of completely wearing out the R.S.S. cross-ply tyres within a few laps. The prototype was then returned to the workshop at Humber Road, where a smaller 4474cc. 2-barrel carburetted V8 was fitted which developed 218 b.h.p. at 5200 r.p.m.

Two more prototypes of the Snipe were fitted with the V8s, as well as an Imperial and a left-hand drive Snipe. However, unreliability problems persisted, with burnt pistons and blown cylinder-head gaskets. The engines were really too powerful for the vehicle to cope, and the prospect of an expensive re-engineering exercise on the bodyshell and components was out of the question. By the time the four-barrel carburettor was replaced with a two, speeds only marginally better than the current "sixes" were achieved with power output of 150 b.h.p. not really very much more powerful than the

This photograph is of a mock-up of the "Sceptre" which in most respects was a new car in its own right. Originally intended to be the Sunbeam Rapier Series IV, it was subsequently decided to market this model as a Humber. The Rapier badging can be clearly seen on the rear wing and the grille on both the mock-up and the pre-production prototype below is from a Sunbeam.

A second styling exercise, similar apart from the treatment of the side flash.

Clearly a pre-production prototype. Note the stick-on ventilation on the wheels and the absence of chrome window surrounds!

Three prototype Sceptres, designated RAP1, RAP2 and RAP3, were built for development work. This interior shot of RAP3, a left-hand-drive version, was taken returning from testing at MIRA. In contrast to the production Sceptre, this prototype had a bench seat.

Left: Production 1.6 litre Humber Sceptre Mark I.

100

The interior of the Mark I Sceptre betrays its Sunbeam origins as a Sports saloon. There is full instrumentation, a floor mounted gearchange, but no trace of the traditional trim of walnut and leather. Nevertheless, the Sceptre was a comfortable and stylish saloon.

Sunbeam Venezia built by Touring Super Leggra of Milan. This was a styling exercise based on the Humber Sceptre floorpan and mechanical components, including an uprated 1592cc Rootes four-cylinder engine. At one stage in 1963, this was considered as a potential candidate for a high performance saloon using a V8 engine. The construction consisted of a tubular spaceframe chassis and aluminium body panels constructed around the floorpan. The interior is based on Hillman saloons, which were built by Touring under licence.

Rear view of the Sunbeam Venetzia.

1965 saw the introduction of the Mark II Sceptre. This featured a more powerful 1725cc engine and a restyled front end and interior trim. This 1965 example was exported to Greece.

129.5 b.h.p. To add to these problems, the engines could only run on 100 octane fuel, which although available, added to the the customer's running costs.

Nevertheless, work continued on the engine and transmission cooling, and rearrangement of the ancillaries was made to create more under-the-bonnet space. A new exhaust system was developed and petrol lines rerouted to separate them from the hot exhaust pipes. Brake pipes were modified. Despite the high fuel consumption and the disappointing performance of the two-barrel version of the 4474cc V8, plans were drawn up to create a pilot production line to build four Super Snipe and two Imperial pre-production cars which would be assembled during March 1966. More problems were encountered. The width of the V8 meant that the engine could only be fitted by dropping it in from above the engine bay, rather than from below, like the standard six-cylinder production engine and gearbox. This did not deter the production team, who scheduled production proper to begin by July 1966. Separate badging was designed, and the V8s were to be identified by a discreet "Humber V8" badge in the front door just below the waist moulding.

In the meantime, the Technical Library issued detailed instructions for the preparation of publicity material on 21st January 1966. However, the project did not go ahead, although six more pre-production cars were built, four Super Snipes and two Sceptres.

By this time Chrysler had taken full control of the Rootes group and decided not to proceed with the project. The costs of commencing production compared with the low projected sales and profits were considered too high and the project was abandoned. As a result no further development work was carried out and the prototypes were sold off. One of the Imperial prototypes was used by Sir Reginald Rootes for some time and is now owned by an official of the Post Vintage Humber Car Club. Other prototypes have been preserved and at least one is now in the United States.

With no further development work undertaken, production of all other "Series" Humbers was discontinued in March 1967 as a result of Chrysler's reorganisation of the Rootes group.

Mark I Sceptre contrasted with Mark II Sceptre.

Rear view of the Mark I Sceptre.

The "Arrow" was the project name for the cars which were intended to replace the various ageing Rootes cars of the mid-1960s. The Hillman Hunter was the first of this range, styled by Rex Fleming, introduced in October 1966. The car in this series of photographs is a prototype Humber, using an uprated 1725cc engine with twin Stromberg carburettors. The interior trim is to a higher specification than the Hillman, having Walnut veneer facia and door-cappings. Reclining Ambla seats were provided and the external detailing and badging was different. Compared to the production Humber Sceptre, the prototype was somewhat dull and unadventurous.

8. DECLINE

A number of factors contributed to the decline of the Rootes Group and to the eventual demise of the Humber marque. The first is clearly related to the control maintained by the Rootes brothers in the 1950s and 1960s. Still ambitious, they made a number of attempts to enlarge the Rootes group in the 1950s, even entering into negotiations with Standard's Alick Dick for a merger in 1955. This was to come to nothing. While a *merger* was endlessly talked about, what William Rootes really had in mind was a *takeover*, and the negotiations floundered on wrangles about the status and seniority of the various directors of both boards following the merger. Later, Sir William drew back from the day-to-day management of the group, but never actually reliquished control. His lack of presence on a day-to-day basis created a vacuum, which was never quite filled because he had failed to groom a similarly talented successor, which, to be fair, would have been a virtually impossible task.

During 1961, industrial relations at the *British Light Steel Pressings* works in Acton deteriorated and in September, an indefinite strike about pay and conditions began. This had an immediate effect on production of Humber bodyshells and other Rootes vehicles, since pressings and sub-assemblies were produced there and then sent to the Ryton plant where they were assembled and painted. The strike dragged on for three months, and though eventually settled on the company's terms, Rootes recorded a loss of £900,000 in 1961 against a profit of £3 million in 1960 and lost over a third of the year's output, which was down by 60,000 units. This was a severe blow. In any case, 1960 and

1961 had seen a slump in car sales. Peter Ware, former chief engineer for the Rootes group, in an interview with *Throughbred and Classic Cars* in September 1988, said *"I'm convinced that the Acton strike of 1961 ruined the company just when we were getting our act together technically."*

A second factor, which affected the fortunes of all the Rootes companies was the development of the Hillman Imp. Why the established Rootes group saw any prospect of making money in the highly competitive small car market was a mystery. Although the production of a small car had been contemplated for some years by the Rootes board, and a number of proposals and prototypes had been put forward, the Imp was rushed through and suffered appalling design and quality control problems in its headlong rush to compete with the BMC Mini. One can speculate whether the decision to introduce the Imp had anything to do with the increasing success of the Volkswagen Beetle, the chance to acquire this having been hastily turned down in 1947. Both were small rear-engined cars and were aimed at similar markets.

With a government moratorium on new factories operating in Coventry, Rootes accepted a greenfield site at Linwood in Glasgow, opposite to a new Pressed Steel plant, which would be dedicated to the new car project. The capital cost of the construction of the Linwood plant was £25 million, to which was added losses through 1962 and 1963. This was a completely new plant with a completely new workforce, which made the whole project alarmingly risky. An untrained workforce assembling a car which had yet to be fully developed resulted

The production Humber Sceptre Mark III. Compared to the prototype, it has more brightwork, higher specification wheeltrims and coachlining.

Close up of the detailing on the Sceptre Mark III production car. The additional guttering brightwork is clearly visible. A vinyl roof has been added together with a "H" badge. At the front, the double headlamps are framed by an aluminium finish panel. Rubber-faced overriders can be seen to the front and rear, as well as the "HUMBER" badges.

in appalling quality control problems and additional expense. Senior Rootes managers were drawn from other parts of the group to deal with this accumulation of problems at a time when the established range of models was in need of continuing updating and development.

To finance this new venture, the group took on a huge government loan. Servicing of this loan was cripplingly expensive, and this resulted in a drain on finances at a time when the company was still trying to recover from the effect of the damaging strike at Acton and it had to borrow funds from its own dealers at one point to prevent imminent collapse.

In addition, the group had no established expertise in the production or selling of small cars, although

development work had been done since the mid-1950s, so expertise was bought in. The new Imp used all-new components, with accompanying problems in build quality and the unfortunate result that the elaborate and expensive casting machinery needed failed to work properly.

Beset with development problems and the timing of the Imp's launch was extremely poor. Already competing with the BMC Mini, it also had to compete with Standard-Triumph and Vauxhall, who were more successful with the Triumph Herald and Vauxhall Viva than Rootes with the Imp, which failed to sell as anticipated. Rootes dealers had no experience in selling small cars and the fact that the Hillman Super Minx and Vogue cars had not been well-received and no radical development

Restyling exercise for 1974. Wheel trims have been modified, new bumpers are fitted front and back with auxilliary lamps incorporated into the bumper. Driving mirrors were standard and the seats now had cloth inserts.

Extract from the Chrysler catalogue of 1973. By this time, the Humber range consisted of one model and a quarter page entry in a 32 page catalogue.

1976 saw a final revamp to the Sceptre and the introduction of the last new Humber model, the Sceptre Estate. Tinted glass now featured on saloons and estates and the estate featured a custom built chrome roof-rack and a rear wash-wipe.

work had been carried out on the Humber range did nothing to help, as they had little which was new to offer their current customers.

William Rootes was not a well man and by 1964, the accumulated effects of years of overwork and old age were taking their toll, and the Rootes Group was clearly losing direction. Meanwhile in the United States, Lynn Townsend, a finance expert, had been dealing with Chrysler's problems and had managed to turn the company around from imminent insolvency to profitability.

Founded in 1925, the Chrysler Corporation was the result of a Walter Chrysler's takeover of the ailing Maxwell Motor Company. Chrysler had risen to President of Buick in previous years and brought with him the most talented of Buick's design and management team. Chrysler was then the U.S.A.'s thirty-first largest motor manufacturer. By 1928, following the takeover of

Dodge, it was the third. Chrysler began a massive expansion programme, setting up subsidiaries in Canada, Belgium and Britain. In the early 1960s, after the takeover of Simca in France, the Chrysler Group was looking for a foothold in Britain, and the ailing Rootes group was an ideal candidate for Townsend's ambitions. An approach was made to Billy Rootes in June 1964, and after lengthy bargaining, Rootes sold 30 percent of the voting shares and 50 percent of the non-voting shares to Chrysler for a total of £12 million. Lord

Dimensions

A Overall length 14' 10½"
B Overall width 5' 8"
C Overall height (unladen) 4' 8¼"
    Overall Height (laden) 4' 4"
D Ground Clearance (unladen) 8¾"
    Ground Clearance (laden) 4½"
E Wheelbase 8' 9"
F Luggage Compartment 21 cu. ft.
G Front Legroom 3' 3"
H Front Headroom 3' 2½"
J Rear Headroom 3' 1"
K Rear Legroom 3' 6"
L Front Shoulder Room 4' 7¼"
M Rear Shoulder Room 4' 7"

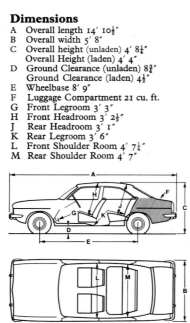

The British Chrysler 180. The last car developed to be a Humber, but badged as a Chrysler.

108

The Chrysler Valiant.

(William) Rootes continued as chairman and Reginald Rootes as deputy. Shortly after the deal was concluded, William Rootes died on 12th December 1964, aged 70.

Reginald Rootes then became chairman and began to address the problems of gradual integration into the Chrysler combine. Chrysler in turn had to deal with the fundamental problems of the Rootes empire. One was the proliferation of models, none of which were particularly profitable. Like many car manufacturers, Rootes had built too many models in the late 1950s and made only small profits per unit. These then lost money in the 1960s as they failed to maintain a competitive edge and costs escalated.

While Chrysler gained majority stake in Rootes from 1964 to 1967, when it's investment amounted to 66% of the equity, it did not gain overall management control. Roy Axe, another ex-Rootes man, formerly of the design team, told *Thoroughbred and Classic Cars* in November 1985 that *"..although a lot of public words were spoken to the effect that Chrysler would not take over the majority shareholding, I think the feeling in the company was that it was inevitable. In fact we in design were looking forward to the takeover because we felt it would benefit our department".* However, when control was finally gained, rather than provide funds for new projects, Chrysler instituted a programme of cutbacks, which included the sale of the troublesome Linwood plant to B.M.C. in 1966 for £14 million.

In April of 1967, Minister of Technology, Anthony Wedgewood Benn, formerly consented to the full takeover of the Rootes group by Chrysler. This resulted in a further injection of £17 million of cash.

At the conclusion of the deal, Reginald Rootes stepped down as chairman and retired. Geoffrey Rootes, son of William Rootes, took over the chair and Gilbert Hunt was brought in from Massey-Ferguson as Managing Director.

The first priority of the new board was to rationalize the combine and they ruthlessly phased out vehicles which failed to meet targets. The ageing big Humbers were amongst these, with market share declining and very low volume production. At the same time the decision was made to close Thrupp & Maberly, which by now was only dealing with the large Humbers. The closure was announced in June 1967, and paint and trim work for the new "Arrow" cars was switched from Cricklewood to Ryton.

The Arrow project represented, in the event, Rootes last sustained attempt to rationalize and modernise it's range of cars. The project was headed by Harry Sheron, who later became group technical director and styling was by Rex Fleming. The Arrow was intended to provide the basis for the Rootes range and to replace the various ageing Hillmans and Humbers.

The first of these to bear the Humber transfer was the Sceptre Mark III, which was intended to be the top-of-the range model with a higher specification of trim. This included a wooden dash, wooden door-trim and centre console together with re-designed p.v.c. reclining seats. The body was of unitary construction in four-door saloon style. The engine was the 1725cc five-bearing engine, fitted with twin Stromberg CD-150 carburettors and coupled to a four-speed, all-syncromesh gearbox with Laycock overdrive on 3rd and top or, as an option, Borg-Warner automatic transmission. This resulted in a moderately fast 98 m.p.h. maximum speed and a typical fuel consumption of some 25 m.p.g. The chassis

The new special edition Solara Sceptre.

The real beauty of it is the price. £5,555.†

And the beauty of the price is that it includes so much. Take a look and you'll see what we mean. A 1600 engine that delivers 40.9 mpg.* Front wheel drive. Power steering. Duotone paintwork Café Noir and Gilt or Fox Grey and Silver. Steel sunroof. Push button radio. Full instrumentation including tachometer. Digital clock. Tinted glass. Laminated windscreen. Remote control driver's door mirror. Front seat head restraints. Tweed cloth seat trim. Reclining front seats. Full wheel trims. Halogen headlamps.

An exceptional list and at £5,555† we're sure you'll agree it has an exceptional price to match. Isn't that beautiful?

TALBOT
TAKES YOU FURTHER
Part of Peugeot S.A. Europe's largest car producer.

†List price excluding road tax, number plates and delivery. *Official DoE figures: Solara Sceptre. At a constant 56 mph – 40.9 mpg (6.9 L/100 km). At a constant 75 mph 31.0 mpg (9.1 L/100 km). Urban Driving 27.7 mpg (10.2 L/100 km).

A Talbot Solara advertisement from 1983. By now the Humber transfers and the model names were the property of Peugeot-Talbot. The "Sceptre" was a limited edition, capitalising on the goodwill attached to the old Humber model name. Similarly, a special edition of the Talbot Horizon was designated the "Pullman".

110

and front suspension utilised Macpherson struts and an anti-roll bar. In external appearance, the Sceptre resembled the contemporary Hillman Hunter, but with a four-headlamp nose.

Some critics were not taken with the new Sceptre, William Boddy described it as:

"..not very nice to drive. The ride is soggy, the steering spongy, low geared and rather heavy, and the ride is lurchy, especially under braking.

"There is plenty of sound damping in the Sceptre but it is not an outstandingly quiet car."

"....the Rover 2000TC is, in my opinion, a more satisfactory purchase."

Nevertheless, the new Humber sold well and the Chrysler group was sufficiently confident in the product to continue to develop the range.

In 1974, an estate version, based on the Hunter Estate, was launched, which was mechanically similar to the saloon. It featured carpetting throughout, including the load deck, a custom fitted roof rack consisting of two chrome longitudinal members with two adjustable cross braces and a rear tailgate wash-wipe system, a relatively advanced feature. Both the saloon and the estate were phased out in February 1976 as a result of the final collapse of Chrysler UK.

There does appear to have been some preliminary thoughts at Chrysler about replacing the Sceptre with a new model. In the late 1960s two models were being developed by Chrysler and Rootes engineers at the Whitley design studio under Roy Axe. One was to become the Hillman Avenger, first introduced in 1971, and the other vehicle was thought to have been planned as a Humber. It was thought that the car would have been offered in two versions, as the new Humber range. According to former Rootes development engineers, the new Humber "Snipe" was intended to be powered by the standard Rootes 1725cc four-cylinder engine, and a new "Super Snipe" was to have been powered by a newly-developed V6 Chrysler engine.

Some prototypes were seen around the Chrysler plant badged as Humbers, but no photographs were taken. The project was dropped in 1969 or 1970 and the production of the base car transferred to the ex-Simca factory at Poissy, near Paris. The car was finally launched in 1971 as the Chrysler 180.

Whilst the Chrysler 180 was the one of the first cars in the United Kingdom to bear the Chrysler name, the Chrysler marque itself was to prove remarkably short-lived. This is possibly because the car-buying public had little perception of what a Chrysler was, other than the vague notion that it was something of American origin. One can only speculate about what may or may not have happened if the corporate planners and marketing executives had persisted with the Humber name.

Peugeot-Talbot acquired the Humber transfers. Although do not have any plans to revive the Humber marque, it is interesting to note that one or two vehicles appeared as limited editions using some of the old Humber model names such as "Sceptre" and "Pullman" in the early 1980s.

There was one odd postscript to the history of Humber in 1987, when one final attempt was made to resurrect the marque.

9. THE BOULTON HUMBER

For a brief period in 1987, an attempt was made to set up a company to recommence production of Humber vehicles. This was the result of efforts by one private individual, Andrew J Boulton, a former marketing manager at the Talbot plant in Linwood, who had formed a new Scottish company, *Humber Motor Company Limited.*

Boulton's plans were remarkably ambitious. He perceived that there was a gap in the luxury car market which was not being filled by British motor manufacturers. He may have been partly correct, Jaguar was a low volume manufacturer and Rover was still developing a range of small luxury cars, although they had replaced the SD1 with the new 800-series. The German BMW and Mercedes were Boulton's "stalking horse", ironically, some 25 years after Rootes had used the Mercedes 220 as a benchmark for the development of the Series Humbers.

On March 27th 1987, he told *The Scotsman:*

"I have thoroughly researched the market and I think that executive and luxury car manufacture is the most profitable sector and that's where I want Humber cars to be."

This was an interesting idea, and oddly enough the 11-year gap between the manufacture of the last Humber Sceptre and his proposals did not appear to deter Boulton. He added that

"Humber cars used to be compared with some of the best in the world in road tests and the name has escaped the problems that have plagued other quality manufacturers in the last decade.

"Initially, I would want two models, a 2.7 litre executive car and 5.4 litre V12 luxury car which could be designed by specialists such as Giugiaro and Porsche and be ready to go into production in about five years."

Boulton's ambitious plans were, however, prevented from coming to fruition by lack of money and suitable premises. £100,000 was, he said, required to present a package for investors, and although potential premises were located at Bathgate, the Rover group, who owned the former Leyland factory, appeared unwilling to sell.

On April 2nd 1987, the Linlithgow *Journal and Gazette* ran an editorial stating that Boulton's plans deserved serious consideration. At the same time further details were revealed of the financial requirements in order to get the scheme off the ground.

"It is anticipated that an initial manufacturing labour force of 2,000 will be required to produce the start-up volume of 10,000 vehicles per year.

It is intended that the facility will be structured to break-even on a single shift capacity of 60,000 vehicles per year. Thus eventually, as many as 10,000

jobs could be created when the annual output hits 200,000 and would put the firm on a comparable footing with Saab, BMW and Volvo."

At this stage, the *Gazette* estimated that as much as £500 million would be needed to bring the plan to fruition. Interviewing George McNiell, then the Director for Planning of West Lothian District Council, McNeill was quoted as saying that:

"..he (Boulton) is being over-optimistic about the scheme; it will take a lot of money to make that plant capable of producing luxury cars."

On 3rd April 1987, the *Lothian Courier* confirmed that the Rover Group had refused to sell the Bathgate plant to Boulton and that Boulton's solicitors were seeking to negotiate with Peugeot-Talbot about the old Humber trade marks. In the meantime, even more ambitious plans were being made. A larger workforce was being contemplated and Boulton was becoming more precise about the companies who were his potential competitors. However, at this point no further progress appears to have been made, and on 7th May 1987, the following press release was made by the Humber Motor Company Limited:

"The new Humber Motor Company Limited is pressing ahead with its proposals to utilise the ex-Leyland Trucks empty Bathgate facility to manufacture:

- "executive" cars, to compete with Saab, Volvo and Ford Granada. - "luxury" cars to compete with BMW 7 Series and Mercedes S Class

"Following encouraging meetings at the end of April 1987, with some of Edinburgh's most successful financiers and entrepreneurs, Mr Andrew J Boulton of the new Humber Motor Company Limited will be seeing the S. D. A. (Scottish Development Authority) during the next week to discuss financing the preparation of the company's business plan.

"The company is confident that the business plan will confirm the viability of the proposal, that eventually could lead to the direct employment of a 10,000 work force, with additional spin-offs in areas of contractors and service sectors.

"The company refused to comment on recent approval by West Lothiam District Council for the alternative "megastore" proposal for the site, but understands that the Lothian Regional Council (who have "called in" the "megastore" plans), will take a wider view considering alternative retail and leisure proposals in the region.

"Beyond the region, the Secretary for State for Scotland with also consider the comprehensive redevelopment proposals for the Clyde Port Authority with the backing of Tarmac, as well as those other

ONE MAN'S DREAM

A LINLITHGOW company is behind a multi-million pound scheme to resurrect the Leyland plant in Bathgate.

And if the dream becomes a reality for businessman Andrew Boulton, a staggering 10,000 new jobs could be in the pipeline.

The new "Humber Motor Company Limited" was registered in Edinburgh last year and if approval for a takeover is given, a new range of high quality cars will be manufactured.

Mr Boulton, who lives in Clarendon Road, Linlithgow, said he intends to compete with Saab, Volvo and the Ford Granada in the "executive" sector and against the new Jaguar XJ40, Mercedes "S" and the BMW 7 in the "luxury" class.

The Rover Group plc, has confirmed its intention to pursue a mega-store/complex proposal for the former truck building facility.

But Mr Boulton hopes the promise of jobs in one of the country's worst blackspots will convince local planning chiefs that his scheme is the more viable.

Could Leyland plant turn out luxury cars?

It is anticipated that an initial manufacturing labour force of 2000 will be required to produce the start-up volume of 10,000 vehicles per year.

It is intended that the facility will be structured to break even on a single-shift capacity of 60,000 vehicles per year. Then eventually, as many as 10,000 jobs could be created when the annual output hits 200,000 and would put the firm on a comparable footing with Saab, BMW and Volvo.

The market which Mr Boulton is aiming at is the USA, Middle East and West Germany.

Andrew Boulton is a marketing specialist and a member of the Institute of Marketing. He began his career in the motor industry by joining Fodens in Sandback. In 1976 he joined Chrysler (UK) Ltd and was based at Linwood before it closed down in 1981. For the last two years he has been exploring, developing and refining proposals to continue Bathgate as a manufacturing facility.

IT COULD COST AS MUCH AS £500 MILLION TO BRING TO FRUITION.

That will include the design and engineering of the two principal models and the purchase and refurbishment of the Bathgate plant. The first car would roll off the assembly line in four or five years.

First objective for the new Linlithgow company is to raise the more modest £100,000 required to produce the formal business plan to be presented to potential investors.

Mr Boulton added: "I am pleased with the support and encouragement we have already received".

Mr George McNeill, director of planning for West Lothian District Council, said: "I have not had the chance of speaking properly with Mr Boulton.

"But I think he is being over-optimistic about the scheme. It will take a lot of money to make the plant capable of producing luxury cars".

MOTORING ON . . .
Linlithgow man Andrew Boulton who is bidding to take over Leyland.

ROVER GROUP VETO AMBITIOUS CAR PLAN

─ By Ken Wallace ─

AN ambitious plan to reopen Bathgate's empty Leyland plant for car manufacture has been knocked back by owners Rover Group.

They are refusing to sell the factory to local businessman Andrew Boulton, whose £500 million scheme would create 2000 jobs there.

EXECUTIVE

Mr Boulton, who lives in Clarendon Road, Linlithgow, was a marketing executive at Chrysler's Linwood plant until its closure in 1981.

Now he has spent two years developing a plan which he believes could eventually lead to a workforce of 10,000 employed

by a company the equal of car companies Saab, BMW or Volvo.

And he plans to revive a famous name of Britian's motoring history — for in August last year he founded the Humber Motor Company Ltd.

A spokesman for Peugeot Talbot confirmed this week that they recently received a letter from Mr Boulton's solicitors, opening talks on the purchase of the old Humber trade mark.

The new cars, if the scheme ever goes ahead, would compete in two main markets.

One would sell in the 'executive sector', com-

peting with Saab, Volvo and the Ford Granada. The other would be a luxury model, competing with the Jaguar XJ40, Mercedes 'S' Class and the new BMW 7 series.

OBVIOUS

In a statement released this week, Mr Boulton said the obvious market for these cars would be the U.S., Europe and the Middle East.

He is now attempting to raise £100,000 for a formal

business plan to present to possible investors.

But the total cost of his scheme — including purchase of the factory, installing robot assembly equipment and development of the two new models — is estimated at around £500 million.

However, the project is unlikely ever to take off as Rover have written to Mr Boulton stating they have no plans to sell the Bathgate plant.

They have also confirmed that they intend to go ahead with their own plan to turn it into a major shopping and leisure centre.

---

proposals in the east being considered by the Lothain Regional Council.

"The viability of the established shopping centres and all these alternative proposals based on established centres of population, could be put in jeopardy by the "megastore" which itself would be vulnerable without a large indigenous population to support it.

"The company did comment that the success of its proposal at Bathgate would generate sufficient income in the area to attract itself retail, leisure and other manufacturing employers to the area, without the necessity for financial inducements or continuing subsidy from companies based in the Midlands.

"The new "Humber Motor Company Limited" has been approached by the Industrial Development Board (I. D. B.) for Northern Ireland, to consider an alternative location for its manufacturing facility. This suggestion will be given serious consideration, although all the preliminary work on the company's proposals has been based on the assumption of utilising the large facility at Bathgate, the residual engineering skills in the town, and excellent lines of communication.

"Note: The new Humber Motor Company Limited is not connected with the old Humber Limited. We do not wish to be associated with them, or the vehicles they produced, and will not be marketing spare parts etc for them."

Boulton's plan to revive the British luxury car manufacturing industry fell by the wayside. Several problems plagued the scheme; lack of finance: an estimated £100,000 appears to have been required just to put

together a detailed proposal. Even if this had been raised, the £500 million needed would have had to be raised from large institutional investors or with their backing. No such backing was forthcoming, the new company had no track record in motor manufacturing, or, indeed, any business at all. Boulton himself had no track record in managing the type of business proposed. A marketing specialist, he had started his career at Fodens, and had worked for Chrysler (UK) at Linwood from 1976 to 1981. The Humber Motor Company Limited had no other directors with any clout with conservative City institutions, and although he was successful in getting press coverage for the scheme, this was confined to local newspapers and a short item in the April 8th edition of *Autocar*.

The next serious problem was lack of premises. Rover's redundant Bathgate plant was identified as a potential site, but other proposals for development of the site had already been made by the time Boulton was attempting to raise finance. Clearly the local authorities had taken the view that development of a retail complex was a more attractive proposition, especially as plans for this proposal had attracted the backing of Tarmac, an established construction firm with the immediate financial resources needed to develop the site.

Another item was the question of the Humber trademarks. Boulton's press release of May 1987 appeared to make it clear that the new company did not wish to be connected with the old Humber company or it's products. This was an odd stance for someone who had publically declared that he was negotiating for the Humber transfers with Peugeot-Talbot and who had taken the trouble to register a company with the Humber name. It is also questionable whether "Humber" was an appropriate name to use in the first place. It was quite true that Humber had not been plagued by quality control problems in the same way as firms such as Jaguar or Rover, but this was because the company had not manufactured a single car since February 1976 which could cause such problems.

However, Boulton's perception of Humber was based on it's days of "the poor man's Rolls-Royce" and the immediate Post-War era. The vehicle of 1976 in 1987 was widely perceived by the wider car-buying public as another dreadful secondhand 1970s car, which was not, even when new, considered to have any great merit in engineering or marketing terms. If Boulton was going to revive a great British marque, Humber may not have been the right one at that time.

It is interesting to note that in 1976, the perspective was quite different from Boulton's. Graham Robson, in an article in the 3rd January 1976 *Autocar* entitled *"The Chrysler Crisis - How Important?"* made the following telling observations:

"Look at the record. Technically, Chrysler had little to offer in Britain. There was the complex cross pollination of skills between Whitley and Carrierres (in Spain) in design and engineering, but the purely British products were dull.....

"What about sales? Once again, a complete end to Hillman, Humber and Sunbeam production would not be a lasting tragedy. Sad but true. The company's market share has been declining for some time. Figures of five or six percent are hardly significant especially when you study those achieved by Datsun, VW, Fiat and Renault in this country merely with an import network...

"To the motorist does it even matter that the British car making league could come down from "Big Four" to "Big Three"?"

Robson could write with some authority. He had been employed by the Rootes group and had observed their decline, both under the Rootes family and Chrysler, at close quarters.

Even if finance could have been raised, even if Boulton could have put together the right development team, even if the marketing campaign had been clever enough, there is the question of whether the new Humber would, with hindsight, ever have made a return for its investors? Boulton himself estimated that four years would have been needed to develop his proposed vehicles. He was probably reasonably realistic in this, if, as proposed, he was to draw on the skills of established manufacturers such as Porsche and provided he was prepared to use tried and tested mechanical components. However, in April 1991, exactly four years on from the initial publicity for the new Humber scheme, representatives from the major motor manufacturing companies were holding urgent talks with Norman Lamont, the Chancellor of the Exchequer, concerned at the worst downturn in trade for over a decade. British luxury car manufacturers have seen a continuing round of redundancies and short-time working in one of the worst recessions since the Second World War. In such a climate, could a new luxury car maker, its products untried, possibly have got off the ground?

APPENDICES

APPENDIX II
ROOTES HUMBERS

Known production figures for the Rootes Humbers are summarised below:

Model		Year	Nos. built.	Remarks
Humber 12 h.p		1933-37	8,486	Discontinued 1937.
Humber 16/60		1932-35	7,891	Replaced by new range of Snipe/80 and Pullman large Humbers
Humber 18 h.p		1935-37	866	
Humber Snipe		1935-37	2,652	Range discontinued 1937 and replaced by new Snipe models.
Humber Pullman		1935-39	3,700	Discontinued 1940. Replaced by new bodystyle. Resumed civilian production 1945
Humber 16 h.p.		1937-39	1,925	Discontinued
Humber Snipe		1939/40	2,706	Renamed Hawk/Snipe/Super Snipe for 1945.
Humber Super Snipe		1938-40	c.1,500	Many built for military use 1939-45. See Appendix (ii) below.
Humber Hawk Mark I		1945-48	Unknown	Discontinued with introduction of Humber Hawk Mark II
Humber Hawk Mark II		1948-50	c.4,000	Updated to Mark III
Humber Super Snipe Mark I		1945-48	3,909	Discontinued with introduction of Mk II
Humber Super Snipe Mark II		1948-50	8,361	Updated to Mark III
Humber Super Snipe Mark III		1950-52	8,703	Succeeded by Mark IV.
Humber Pullman Mark I		1945-48	Unknown	Succeeded by Mark II
Humber Pullman Mark II		1948-51	c.2,200	Succeeded by Mark III
Humber Pullman Mark III		1951-53	1,526	Succeeded by Mark IV
Humber Imperial Mark II, III & IV		1949-53	Unknown	Same specification as Pullman, but without limousine division.
Humber Pullman Mark IV		1953-54	414	Discontinued 1954. No replacement introduced.
Humber Hawk Mark III		1948-50	10,040	Succeeded by Mark IV
Humber Hawk Mark IV		1950-52	6,942	Succeeded by Mark V
Humber Hawk Mark V		1952-54	c.14,300	Succeeded by Mark VI
Humber Hawk Mark VI		1954-55	18,836	
Humber Hawk Mark VIA		1955-57	9,614	Discontinued and replaced by Humber Hawk Series I
Humber Super Snipe: Mark IV		1952-54	9,785	
	Mark IVA	1954-55	676	
	Mark IVB	1955-57	7,532	Replaced by Super Snipe Series I
Humber Hawk:	Series I	1957-59	15,539	
	Series IA	1959-60	6,813	
	Series II	1960-62	7,230	
	Series III	1962-64	6,109	
	Series IV	1964-65	1,746	
	Series IVA	1965-67	3,754	Discontinued, not replaced.
Humber Super Snipe: Series I		1958-59	6,072	
	Series II	1959-60	7,175	
	Series III	1960-62	7,257	
	Series IV	1962-64	6,495	
	Series V	1964-65	1,907	
	Series VA	1965-67	1,125	Discontinued, not replaced.
Humber Sceptre: Mark I		1963-65	17,011	
	Mark II	1965-67	11,985	Discontinued.
	Mark III ("Arrow")	1967-76	43,951	Last Humber built, February 1976.

APPENDIX III
HUMBER GOVERNMENT VEHICLES

These have been collected in a separate listing. During 1939 the Ministry of Supply commenced ordering Humber cars for War Department service and appear to have taken virtually every car produced by the factory during the war. Like the civilian chassis numbers, the first number indicates engine type, the second number indicates year of manufacture and the third number indicates body style.

The final four digits are the production run numbers.

Description	Chassis No's.	Description	Chassis No's.
Humber Hawk Staff Saloon	2710009 - 2720001	Super Snipe Utility	8101250 - 8101349
Humber Hawk Staff Saloon	2720049 - 2720066	Super Snipe Utility	8200701 - 8201856
Humber Snipe Staff Saloon	4710007	Super Snipe Utility	8200857 - 8201656
Humber Snipe Staff Saloon	4720001 - 4720010	Super Snipe Utility	8201657 - 8202173
Humber Snipe Utility	5002115 - 5002464	Super Snipe Staff Saloons	8202201 - 8202700
Staff Pullmans	6200515 - 6200516	Super Snipe Wireless & Personnel	8202701 - 8204200
Staff Pullmans	6200520 - 6200529	Super Snipe Utility	8204301 - 8204776
Staff Pullmans	6200531 - 6200549	Super Snipe Utility	8216201 - 8216402
Staff Pullmans	6200551 - 6200719	Super Snipe L.R.C.	8240001 - 8240229
Staff Pullmans	6200750 - 6200763	Super Snipe L.R.C. Mark II	8240301 - 8240700
Staff Pullmans	6200791 - 6200801	Super Snipe L.R.C. Mark II	8241301 - 8241500
Staff Pullmans	6210501 - 6210538	Super Snipe Utility	8250001 - 8251423
Staff Pullmans	6210551 - 6210562	Super Snipe Staff Saloon	8260001 - 8262627
Staff Pullmans	6210571 - 6210637	Super Snipe Personnel	8270001 - 8270500
Staff Pullmans	6210726 - 6210751	Super Snipe Wireless	8280001 - 8281000
Staff Pullmans	6400001 - 6400012	Super Snipe Wireless	8281201 - 8281700
Staff Pullmans	6410031 - 6410042	Super Snipe Tourer	8290001 - 8390300
Staff Pullmans	6410051 - 6410075	Super Snipe F.W.D. Heavy Utility	8350001 - 8351215
Staff Pullmans	6420001 - 6420016	Super Snipe L.R.C. Mark II & IIIA	8360001 - 8360400
Staff Pullmans	6420021 - 6420027	Super Snipe L.R.C. Mark II & IIIA	8360501 - 8361700
Staff Pullmans	6430001 - 6430154	Super Snipe F.W.D. Personnel	8370351 - 8370695
Staff Pullmans	6430301 - 6430441	Super Snipe Wireless	8380346 - 8380550
Staff Pullmans	6430480 - 6430404	Super Snipe F.W.D. Ambulance	8390001 - 8390340
Staff Pullmans	6430501 - 6430999	Super Snipe F.W.D. Ambulance	8390381 - 8390580
Staff Pullmans	6500501 - 6520525	Super Snipe Heavy Utility	8450001 - 8452720
Staff Pullmans	6510501 - 6510579	Super Snipe L.R.C. Mark II & IIA	8460001 - 8461200
Staff Pullmans	6600501 - 6600720	Super Snipe Ambulance	8490726 - 8490731
Staff Pullmans	6630501 - 6600720	Scout	8530001 - 8533998
Staff Pullmans	6710005/14/26/28/32/36/38	Scout	8535001 - 8535300
Staff Pullmans	6710051/53/61/68/95	Super Snipe F.W.D. Heavy Utility	8550001 - 8551009
Staff Pullmans	6720054 - 6720071	Super Snipe F.W.D. Heavy Utility	8650501 - 8654611
Staff Pullmans	6720090 - 6720103/104	Super Snipe Staff Saloons	8660101 - 8660900
Staff Pullmans	6740162/166/170/178	Super Snipe Tourer	8690101 - 8690150
Super Snipe Utility	5002115 - 5002484	Super Snipe Staff Saloon	8710100 - 8710103
Super Snipe Utility	8101156 - 8101171	Super Snipe Staff Saloon	8720001 - 8720056

119

APPENDIX IV
THE POST-VINTAGE HUMBER CAR CLUB

Recognised by Peugeot-Talbot Limited and a founder member of the Association of Rootes Car Clubs, the Post Vintage Humber Car Club was formed after an inaugural meeting on 7th December 1974 by ten enthusiasts. The club has since grown to 1,500 enthusiasts worldwide in the Britain, the U.S.A., Australia, New Zealand, the Far East and Europe.

There is a quality bi-monthly magazine "Old Faithful", named after Field-Marshall Montgomery's Humber Snipe staff car, which won the Thoroughbred and Classic Cars Club Magazine of the Year Award in 1983.

Social activities include a number of rallies throughout the year, often in conjunction with other clubs, with various competitions and concours events at the annual National Rally. Monthly meetings are held at local level and are a focal point for the exchange of information and local social activities.

There is a Club Spares Scheme, run by volunteers, which manages to fulfill some 90% of requests for parts, and holds a large stock of parts for the various post-1930 Humbers.

An assistance scheme, HUMBERHELP, exists to help members whose cars break down far from home. There is a special motor insurance scheme for members, and R.A.C. membership is available at reduced rates.

Further details and applications for membership can be made by writing to:

2 Melton Court
Havelock Road
Croydon
Surrey
CR0 6QQ

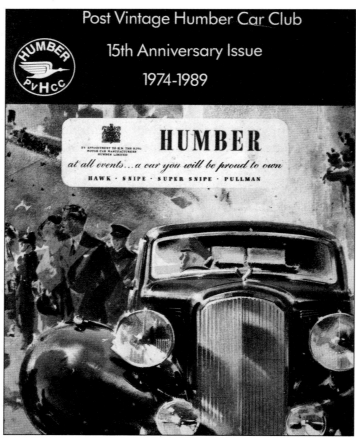

"Old Faithful", prize-winning magazine of The Post Vintage Humber Car Club.

APPENDIX V
THE HUMBER REGISTER

After an inaugural meeting on 1 April 1951, The Humber Register was formed and is dedicated to the preservation of pre-1932 Humber cars. With a comprehensive spares operation and a worldwide membership of 300, the Register has had remarkable success over the years in finding and preserving veteran and vintage Humber cars. There is an active spares operation, a bi-monthly magazine, rallies and a monthly social meeting in London.

Further details and applications for membership can be made by writing to:

Lt Col. Richard Arman
Northbrook Cottage
175 York Road
Broadstone
Dorset
BH18 8ES
Telephone: 0202 695937

APPENDIX VI
OTHER HUMBER AND RELATED CAR CLUBS

The Salmons Tickford Enthusiasts Club
93 Tickford Street
Newport Pagnell
Bucks
MK16 9AW

Humber Car Club of Australia
PO Box 272
North Paramatta 2151
New South Wales
Australia

Humber Car Club of Victoria
23 High Street
Watsonia 3087
Victoria
Australia

Humber Car Club of South Austarlia
4 Williams Crescent
Linden Park 5065
South Australia

Humber Car Club of Queensland
5 Solway Street
Carina 4152
Queensland
Australia

Humber Car Club of Western Australia
PO Box 565
Kalamunda 6076
Western Australia

Rootes Group Car Club of Victoria Inc.
PO Box 932
Glen Waverley
3150 Victoria
Australia

Humber Car Club of Tasmania
7 Magnet Street
Launceston
Tasmania 7250

Humber-Hillman Car Club of New Zealand
31 Swaffield Road
Papatoetoe
Auckland
New Zealand

The Rootes Car Club of Belgium
Ryenlanddreef 31 (BBL)
2060 Merksem
Antwerpen
Belguim

INDEX

References to Illustrations are in italics.

A

Airflow Streamline   81
Armstrong Siddeley   85
Arroll-Johnstone   19
Aston   39
Autocar   8, 11, 31, 37, 39, 43, 44, 47, 66, 90, 118
Avro   *26,* 28
Axe   111, 112

B

B.B.C.   47, 49, 50, 82
Baxter, Raymond   87, 93
Bentley   24
Bentley, W O   24
Benz   6, 11
Benz, Karl   6
Biggs, T J   22, 23
Black, John   29, 31
Bleriot Monoplane   22, *23*
Blue Riband   76, 78, 85
BMW   6, 112
Boddy, William   86, 111
Bollee   11, 16
Bollee, Leon   11
Boulton, Andrew   112. *113,* 114
Bristol   46
Bristol-Siddeley   85
British Light Steel Pressings   81, 94, 105
British Motor Corporation   6, 105, 106
British Motor Syndicate Limited   6, 10
Brooklands   24
Buick   6, 31, 44, 97, 107
Burford, H G   22
Burgess, Frederick   24, 39

C

Campion, William   6, 7
Carbodies   82
Carter, R M   66
Castle Bodies   *59,* 68
Chevrolet   81, 82
Chrysler   31, 43, 89, 92, 97, 99, 102, 107, 109, 111, 114
Chrysler 180 108
Chrysler Valiant 109
Churchill, Winston   46, 48, *53,* 80
Clement   18
Clyno   29
Coatalen, Louis   18, 19, 21
Cole, J A   22, 24, 25, 29, 33, 36
Commer   29, 33, 40, 50, 76, 85
Cooper, Frederick   7, *8*
Crowden, Charles   18

Cutts, John   78

D

Daimler   6, 8, 10, 15, 43, 49, 50, 90, 97
Daimler, Gottleib   6, 8
De Dion Bouton   17
De Normanville   *38,* 40, 94
De Normanville, Captain E   40
Demaus, Brian   3, 17, 116
Devonshire House   29, 47
Dick, Alick   105
Dodge   51
Dowding, Sir Hugh   46
Dynamax   40, 44

E

Edinburgh Rally   68
Evans, P J   12
Evenkeel   40, *40,* 42, 43, 58, 59

F

Fairbanks, Douglas   43
Falconer, Hon Ion Keith   7
Fiat   114
Fison, C H   43

G

Gastonides, Maurice   61
General Motors   25, 33
Gordon Bennett Trophy   19
Gray, Michael   46
Great Horseless Carriage Company   16

H

Hancock, Bill   78
Heath, George Limited   29
Heynes, William   31
Hicks, Mr, first Humber car customer   *16,* 17 *(car 15)*
Hillman   21, 29, 31, 33, 36, 39, 40, 58, 81, 92, 94, 99, 109, 114
    Avenger   111
    Hunter   111
    Imp   105
    William   29
    Wizard   *31,* 35
Hinchcliffe, B C   80
Hinde, Ballin   22
Hooley, Ernest T   7, 8, 10, 11, 17
Hudson   43, 44
Humber
    4 ½ h.p *17*
    10 h.p.   22, 24, *26, 27,* 37
    10/12 h.p.   *18, 20, 22,* 19, 20
    10/14 h.p.   22
    11 h.p.   6, *25*

11.4 h.p. *14*, 25, *27*, 28
11.9 h.p. 23
12 h.p. (early type) *17*, 18, 19, 22, *24*
12/25 28, *28*
14 h.p. 22, 23, 24, *25, 26*, 37
14/40 29
15 h.p. 22
15 h.p. Touring Car 20
15.9 h.p. 25, 26, *26*
15/40 28
16 h.p. Touring Car 24
16/20 h.p. 19, 20
16/60 *34*, 37, *38*, 39, 42
20 h.p. (early type) 19, *23*, 24
20/55 28, *30*
20/65 30, 34
20/70 31
28 h.p. 22, 23
8 h.p. (early type) 22
8 h.p. Light Car 26
8/10 h.p. 19
9/20 Tourer 28
8/18 28
Armoured Car *47*, 48
B.B.C. Recording Van 48
BR-2 Engines 26
Coventry Military Vehicle 50
3½ h.p. 17
Eighteen 42
FV1600 series 51, *51, 52*, 52
Hawk
   Mark I *54*, 58
   Mark II 58
   Mark III 59
   Mark IV *60*, 59, *66, 68*, 76, *78*
   Mark IVA 78
   Mark IVB 77
   Mark V 80
   Series I 81, 82, *84, 85, 86, 88, 89*
   Series IA 85
   Series II 86, *89, 91*
   Series III 87, *93*
   Series IV 92, *94, 96*
Heavy Utility 47
Hexanaut 50
Humberette *18*, 19, 20, 22, 23, 24, 48
Imperial 35, 36, 68
   Series cars 90, *96*, 97
   V8 99, 102
Ironside 48
Light Reconnaissance Car 49
Motor Cycles
   2¾ h.p. 12
   3½ h.p. single-cylinder 12
   4½ h.p. Flat Twin 12, *12, 13, 14*
   5½ h.p. 12
   Olympia Tandem 12
   Olympia Tricar 11
   Standard Special 12
   Voiturette 11, 17
"Pig" 52, *52*
Pullman

Forces vehicle 47
   Mark I *55*, 57, 58
   Mark II *55, 57*, 59, 61, 68
   Mark III *61, 68*, 68
   Mark IV 76
   Mulliner-bodied *56*, 59
   Pre-War 6, *32*, 34, 36, *38*, 39, *41*, 43, 44, *45*
Sceptre
   Mark I 94, *100, 101, 103*
   Mark II 94, 102
   Mark III *104-107*, 109, 111
   V8 97, 99
Scout Car 49, *49*
Sixteen 43, 44, *45*
Snipe 80 37
Snipe Imperial 43
Snipe, Pre-War *32, 33, 36*, 40, *41*, 42, 43, 44, *44, 45*, 46, *46*
Snipe Staff Car 46, *47*, 50
Spider Bicycle 7
Super Snipe
   Mark I *53, 54, 55*, 57, 58, 59
   Mark II *58, 59*, 61, *65*, 66
   Mark III *62, 63*, 66, 68
   Mark IV *69*, 76, *79*, 80
   Mark IVA 80
   Pre-War 44, 46
   Prototype Series Cars 81, 82, 83
   Series I 85, 86, *86, 87, 88*
   Series II 86, *90*
   Series III 86, 87, *90, 91, 92*
   Series IV 87, *92, 93*
   Series V 89, *93, 95, 97, 99*
   V6 111
   V8 *98*, 99, 102
   Twelve *34, 35*, 37, 39, 40, *41*
   Vogue *33*, 40, 106
Humber, Thomas 6, 7, *8*, 16
Hunt, Gilbert 109

I
Irving, Captain John 31
Issigonis, Alec 43
Itala 29

J
Jaguar 31, 90, 112, 114
Johnson, Leslie 78

K
Kane-Pennington 11, 16
Karmann 50, *51*
Keens 34

L
Lambert, Thomas 7, *8*
Lamont, Norman 114
Lanchester 8, 15, 48
Lawson, Harry J 6, 8, 10, 11, 15, 16, 17, 18
Leese, Sir Oliver 46
Leonard, William 66
Linlithgow Journal and Gazette 112
Longman, C A 80

Lothian Courier, The   112

M
Maberly, George   34
Massey-Ferguson   109
Maudslay, Reginald   29
Maxwell Motor Company   107
May, Sir George   29
McNiell, George   112
Mercedes   22, 89, 112
Michaux   6, 7
Milnes-Daimler   22
Minchin, R P   66
MIRA   99
Modern Motoring   39, 42
Monte Carlo Rally   66, 80
Montgomery, Field Marshall   46, *47,* 47, 120
Morris   29, 50, 86
Morris, William   33
Moss, Stirling   78, 80
Motor Cycle, The   12
Motor Sport   86, 94
Mulliner   59
Museum of British Road Transport   47

N
Neagle, Anna   43
Noble, Dudley   40, 42

P
Panhard   11, 18, 66
Pennington   10, 11, 15, 16
Pennington, E J   6, 10, 15, 18
Peugeot   24
Peugeot-Talbot   111, 112, 113, 120
Phelon and Moore   11, 12
Phillips, Walter   16, 21
Police   66, 93
Post Vintage Humber Car Club   120
Powell, Edward   7, 16, 21
Powell, George   17
Pressed Steel   105
Pressed Steel Company   33, 58
Pullinger, T C   19, 23
Pullman
     Peugeot-Talbot, use of name   111

R
RAC   87, 93
Raleigh   8, 13, 29
Rambler   90
Red Flag Acts   15
Renault   114
Robson, Graham   114
Rootes, Company   6, 8, 13, 25, 29, 33
Rootes, Brain   53
Rootes Distributors   29
Rootes' Gazette   *42,* 43
Rootes, Geoffrey   53, 109
Rootes, Reginald   29, 33, *89,* 102, 109
Rootes, William   29, 33, 46, 53, 79, 105, 107
Rover   90, 94, 97, 111, 112
Rucker, Martin   7, 10, 11, ·16, 17
Rudge   7, 16

Rushforth-Marriott, Thomas   7
Russell, Lord   21, 22

S
Saab   112
Saltburn Speed Trials   24
Scotsman, The   112
Sedgwick, Michael   6, 78
Shacklock, C H   17
Shadow Factory Scheme   46
Shelsley Walsh   24
Sheron, Harry   109
Simms, Frederick   8, 15
Snipe Mascot   *36,* 43
SS Cars   31
Standard   29, 31, 48, 105
Standard-Triumph   106
Stanley Show   17
Studebaker   40, 42, 90
Sturmey, Henry   8
Sunbeam   29, 81, 87, 94, 97, 99, 114
Sunbeam-Talbot   80

T
Talbot Solara Sceptre   110
Tangent & Coventry Cycle Company   8
Tarring, John   17, 116
The Motor   26, 43, 44, 58, 59, 68, 86
Thoroughbred & Classic Cars   109, 120
Thrupp & Maberly   29, 31, 34, 39, 40, 44, *44,* 46,
     47, 59, 61, 90, 109
Todd Motors   58
Townsend, Lynn   107
Triumph   106
Tuck, W G   24

V
Valiant   89, 92, 93
Vauxhall   106
Volkswagen   50, 51, 105
Volvo   112

W
Ware, Peter   88, 105
Wedgewood-Benn, Anthony   109
Weymann   30, 34, 35
Wilde, Alfred   31
Windsor, HRH Duke of (formerly King Edward VIII)   43
Wright, Sam   24
Wyand, Paul   46
Wyburn   34

Y
York, HRH Duke of (later King George VI)   43, 53

ABOUT THE AUTHOR

Tony Freeman was born in Middlesbrough in 1961, and comes from a family which has been involved in the motor trade since before the First World War. Having worked as a company secretary for several publicly-quoted companies, he is now a full-time author, director of a publishing company and editor of a club magazine, with occasional freelance work.

Author of books on Daimler, Lanchester, Humber and Standard, he is currently working on a documentary about the early history of recorded sound and a humorous book on the UK banking system.

A name becoming well known to transport enthusiasts all over the world, **Academy Books** is the publisher of high quality, good value specialist books on motorised transport.

To place an order write to:
Academy Books Limited
35 Pretoria Avenue
London E17 7DR

or telephone: **081 521 7647**
or fax: **081 503 6655.**

All major credit cards are accepted.

Daimler and Lanchester An Illustrated History
by Tony Freeman
ISBN: 1 873361 01 7 £19.95
A4 hardback, 144pp, 200 illustrations
Foreword by Bill Hayden, Chairman, Jaguar Cars

From obscure origins in a Cannstatt workshop, Daimler grew to be one of the greatest of Britain,s motor manufacturers. Lanchester, meanwhile, was to the forefront of technology, but failed to achieve any commercial success. Amalgamating in 1931, a tradition of innovation and craftsmanship through the Second World War and beyond.
"Academy Books are a new motoring publisher producing the the type of books that will be of serious interest to MOTOR SPORT readers"
William Kimberley
Motor Sport
"A landmark work on two historic marques, which is an enjoyable read, and a valuable reference."
Les Hughes
Australian Jaguar
"A good informative read."
Brian Kennedy
AutoClassic

Lanchester Cars 1895-1956
Tony Freeman
ISBN: 1873361 00 9 £11.95
A4 softback, 112pp, 190 illustrations

The first publication of its kind devoted to this illustrious marque, bringing together the previously unpublished recollections of Frederick and George Lanchester, transcripts of Maurice Platt's Lanchester Lectures and the discovery and restoration of the very last Lanchester car. Rare photographs and manuscripts and reprints from top contemporary motoring journals are included on this great British marque.
"The first book on Lanchester for over 25 years and what an excellent publication this is...an absolute must for anyone who wants to learn about Lanchester."
Malcolm McKay
Classic Cars

How to Trace the History of Your Car
A Guide to Motor Vehicle Registration Records in Great Britain, Ireland, the Isle of Man and the Channel Islands.
Philip Riden
ISBN: 1 873361 05 X £3.95
80pp softback

Philip Riden explains how the motorist goes about verifying the history of his vehicle. With a comprehensive survey covering the whole of the UK and Ireland, a directory of registration marks, addresses and telephone numbers is included of where surviving records can be found.
"Comprehensive, useful and bang up to date."
AutoClassic
"What a splendid little book! Ever since the DVLC was set up at Swansea with its notorious computer, there were rumours of former county records ..."
"He provides all the information you need to trace the records for your car. It works."
"I recommend this book wholeheartedly."
Malcolm McKay
Classic Cars

Pre-War Standard Cars, 1903 - 1940
Compiled by Brian Long and Tony Freeman
ISBN: 1 873361 02 5 £10.95
A4 softback, 112 pages, 200 illustrations

"I want my car to be composed purely of those components whose principles have been tried and tested and accepted as reliable standards, in fact, I will name my car the Standard car."
Reginald Walter Maudslay, 1903
By 1924 Standard's output was only matched by Austin and their cars enjoyed continued success during the 1930s with the introduction of the very popular and successful "Flying Standards". Standard cars were cheap, unpretentious and reliable. A collection of articles, road tests, manufacturer's brochures and performance data has been assembled, together with an abridged history of the Standard company.